AF663137

THE ARCHAEOLOGY OF MIDDLE GANGA PLAIN

NEW PERSPECTIVES

(Excavations at Agiabir)

THE ARCHAEOLOGY OF MIDDLE GANGA PLAIN

—— NEW PERSPECTIVES ——

(Excavations at Agiabir)

PURUSHOTTAM SINGH
ASHOK KUMAR SINGH

INDIAN INSTITUTE OF ADVANCED STUDY
SHIMLA

ARYAN BOOKS INTERNATIONAL
NEW DELHI

THE ARCHAEOLOGY OF MIDDLE GANGA PLAIN
NEW PERSPECTIVES
(Excavations at Agiabir)

ISBN-81-7305-267-0

© **Indian Institute of Advanced Study, Shimla**

All rights reserved. No part of this book may be reproduced, utilised in any form or by any means, electronic and mechanical, including photocopying, recording or by any information storage and retrieval system without permission in writing from the publishers.

First Published in **2004** by

INDIAN INSTITUTE OF ADVANCED STUDY
Rashtrapati Nivas, Shimla-171005
and
ARYAN BOOKS INTERNATIONAL
Pooja Apartments 4B, Ansari Road, New Delhi-110 002 (India)
Tel.: 23287589, 23255799; Fax : 91-11-23270385; E-mail aryanbooks@vsnl.com

Computer Typeset at ABI Prints & Publishing Co., New Delhi
Printed in India at B.B.N. Printers, New Delhi

Foreword

It was earlier considered that the Aryan culture spread in the Mid-Ganga Valley in the later Vedic period when *Videghamadhava* brought the fire from the banks of the great river Saraswati and crossed river Sarayu. Historians also used to talk about the history of this region from the sixth century BC only with the origins of Buddhism and Jainism and the beginning of the second urbanization, the first being the Indus civilization. The entire scenario changed from 1960 onwards, thanks to the efforts of late Prof. G.R. Sharma who headed a team of scholars of the Department of Ancient History, Culture and Archaeology of Allahabad University and excavated various sites in this area. He had made a singular contribution in unravelling the pre- and protohistoric cultures of the Mid-Ganga Valley.

The Mid-Ganga Valley has played a significant role in the emergence of early farming communities. Excavations carried out at Chopani Mando, Sarai Nahar Rai, Mahadaha and Warikalan-Damdama (all Mesolithic) and Koldihwa, Mahagara, Tokwa, Jhusi and Lahuradeva (all Neolithic) have produced evidence of the gradual evolution of village life in this region. The available evidence suggests that the Mesolithic man started cultivating wild rice in the area and started domesticating certain wild animals. Thus he had reached the threshold of the Neolithic Revolution. The Mesolithic phase in the Middle Ganga Valley has been tentatively assigned a time-bracket of 10,000-5,000 BC.

Breeding of selected wild animals and cultivation of selected wild grasses (rice) marked the succeeding phase of human evolution, termed Neolithic. The sedentary way of life and production of surplus food was a great landmark in the march towards civilization and changed the course of human history. Evidence for the cultivation of rice comes from the Neolithic levels of Koldihwa and Lahuradeva, which has been dated to the later half of the sixth millennium BC.

The Sarayupar region of the Mid-Ganga Valley is equally rich in archaeological sites. The first site to be excavated in the area was Sohagaura, 30 km to the south of Gorakhpur city at the confluence of Rapti (ancient Achiravati) and Ami (ancient Anoma) by the Department of Ancient History, Culture and Archaeology, Gorakhpur University in 1962-63. For the first time painted Black-and-Red Ware pottery was reported in this area above the Neolithic levels, along with the Painted Grey Ware pottery. Later on Prof. Purushottam Singh excavated another site called Narhan on the banks of Ghaghara and christened this particular Painted Black-and-Red Ware of the area as 'Narhan ware'.

Prof. Singh has done a commendable work in carrying out a 'limited excavation' at Agiabir. He has very carefully recorded the cultural sequence of the site from 1300 BC onwards. The report is well documented and shows the regional variations in case of Black-and-Red Ware found at Agiabir and other sites. The finding of a *lota* is unique, as it has not been reported from any other site in the Sarayupar region. The rich find of terracotta discs, metal tools, lamp-stands, etc., make the site all the more important. The finding of microliths and beads at Agiabir, which was absent from all other sites of the Sarayupar plains, too is an important finding and has the potential to influence future research in the area.

The excavators-authors of the report on the excavation of Agiabir deserve to be congratulated for their sincere efforts in publishing the results of their excavation, as it is a rare phenomenon these days. Excavations conducted at important sites some three to four decades earlier are yet not reported.

G.C. Pande

Preface

This book embodies a summary account of the archaeological excavations carried out at Agiabir during 1998-2000 by the authors, on behalf of the Banaras Hindu University. This ancient settlement is situated on the left bank of the Ganga in district Mirzapur in eastern Uttar Pradesh. This investigation has provided a culture sequence of about two thousand years ranging in date from *c.* 1500 BC to AD 700. This long story of human civilization in the Mid-Ganga Valley has been divided into five periods. A glance at this report will show that many hitherto unrecorded facets of human civilization had remained undocumented so far. Sometimes we wonder that how such a huge township extending for a kilometre and a half along the Ganga, remained unnoticed in an area where intensive fieldwork is going on for almost half a century.

The Archaeology of Middle Ganga Plain : New Perspectives (Excavations at Agiabir) is not an excavation report written in traditional style but gives a synoptic view of the main results in the backdrop of the progress made in the archaeology of the Middle Ganga Valley till today. We hope that it will be useful to the serious students of archaeology as well as historians of ancient India and general readers alike.

Contents

Foreword *v*
Preface *vii*
Acknowledgements *xi*
List of Illustrations *xiii*

1. THE MIDDLE GANGA PLAIN **1**
The Land 1
The Drainage System 3
The Flora 5
Culture-Sequence 6
Iron Age 15

2. RESULTS OF AGIABIR EXCAVATIONS **19**
Location and Discovery of the Site 23
Strata, Periods and Pottery 23
Period II (Pre-NBPW with Iron) 34
Period III (NBPW Period) 37
Period IV (Sunga-Kushana Period) 39
Period V (Gupta and Post-Gupta Deposits) 42

3. METAL OBJECTS **49**
Copper 49
Iron 49
Cultural Context 51
Analysis of Objects 63

4. SEALS AND SEALINGS **65**

5. OTHER FINDS **69**

The Lithic Industry 69
Beads 72
Bone Points 76
Hopscotches 77
Gamesmen 78
Skin rubbers 78
Terracotta Discs 78
Terracotta Figurines 79

6. EPILOGUE **81**

Bibliography *85*
Index *91*

Acknowledgements

It was in October 2001 that the senior author had an occasion to visit the Indian Institute of Advanced Study, Shimla and deliver a lecture on the excavations at Agiabir. The present text forms the extended version of this lecture. We are grateful to the then foresighted and dynamic Director of this Institute, Prof. V.C. Srivastava for taking a keen interest in the publication of this book on behalf of the Institute.

We are also grateful to the Director-General, Archaeological Survey of India for granting permission to conduct archaeological excavations at Agiabir as also for giving generous financial assistance for this purpose. We are thankful to Prof. Y.C. Simhadri, Vice-chancellor, the Registrar and the Finance Officer, Banaras Hindu University, for providing encouragement and administrative support. We would like to thank Prof. Vidula Jayaswal, Head, Department of AIHC & Archaeology, Banaras Hindu University for extending necessary administrative support. In the field we have received all help and support from Dr R.N. Singh, technical officer in the Department and Dr Santosh Kumar Singh, research fellow, ICHR. B.K. Sinha, the photographer, Ram Badan Ram, the surveyor, A.K. Pandey and Shiva Kumar, both draughtsmen in the Department of AIHC & Archaeology also assisted in the field. Dr Rakesh Tewari, Director, UP State Archaeological Department visited our site and provided administrative support. In addition, he and his colleagues—Girish Chandra Singh, Aribaran Singh Katiyar and Din Dayal Varma helped us in consolidating and lifting the metal objects found during excavation in May 2001.

During the course of excavations, Agiabir was visited by a number of scholars from different parts of the country, namely, V.N. Misra (Pune), V.D. Misra (Allahabad), K.Thimma Reddy (Visakhapatanam), M.D.N. Sahi (Aligarh), S.M.Mishra (Lucknow), Samresh Bandopadhyay (Calcutta),

V.H. Sonawane (Vadodara), Sadashiv Pradhan (Sambalpur), C. Margabandhu (New Delhi), J.N. Pal (Allahabad), Sitaram Dubey (Ujjain) and M.C. Gupta (Allahabad).We have greatly benefited from their scholarly observations.

We are deeply beholden to the doyen of Indologists, Prof. G.C. Pande, Chairman, Governing Body, Indian Institute of Advanced Study for blessing this monograph by writing a Foreword. We express our sincere thanks to Prof. Bhuvan Chandel, Director, Indian Institute of Advanced Study for taking keen interest in the publication of this monograph. Shri A.K. Sharma, Public Relation Officer, has sorted out all our difficulties regarding the publication of this monograph and our sincere thanks are due to him. Our sincere thanks are also due to Shri Vikas Arya of M/s Aryan Books International for publishing this work in elegant manner.

Shimla
Deepavali, 25 October, 2003

Purushottam Singh
Ashok Kumar Singh

List of Illustrations

FIGURES AND LINE DRAWINGS

1. Archaeological sites in the Middle Ganga Plain.
2. Location map of Agiabir.
3. Contour plan of Agiabir.
4. Section of trenches YE6 III & IV.
5. Bowls and basins of Black-and-Red Ware, Period I.
6. Bowls and basins of Black-and-Red Ware, Period I.
7. Black Slipped Ware and Red Ware, Period I.
8. Red Ware, Periods I & II.
9. Grey Ware, Black Slipped Ware, NBP Ware and Red Ware, Period III.
10. Red Ware, Period IV.
11. Votive tank, *Karāhī*, carinated *hāndī* and lipped basin of Red Ware, Period IV.
12. Red Ware, bottle-necked jars and sprinklers, Period IV
13. Red Ware, Period V.
14. Red Ware, Period V.
15. Red Ware, Period V.
16. Cooking vessel (*Hāndā*) of copper, Period III.
17. Cooking vessel (*Hāndā*) of copper, Period III.
18. Cooking vessel (*Hāndā*) of copper, Period III.
19. Copper vessels and mirror, Period III.
20. Iron swords, Period III.

21. Lamp stand of iron, Period III.
22. Microliths of Agiabir, Period I.

PLATES

I. A. General view of the mounds.
B. Excavated trenches on mound–1.
II. A. Silo for storage of grains, Period I.
B. Bead manufacturing workshop, Period I.
III. A. Unfinished stone beads, Period I.
B. Unfinished stone beads of Periods II & III.
IV. A. Rammed floor with post-holes, Period II.
B. Rammed floor of Period III.
V. A. Painted NBP Ware, Period III.
B. Dish of NBP Ware, Period III.
VI. A. Vases of Red Ware with applique designs, Period III.
B. General view of structures, Period IV.
VII. A. View of a room with floor, Period IV.
B. A view of Room No. 1, Period IV.
VIII. A. A view of the same from the east, Period IV.
B. A room of burnt bricks of Period IV.
IX. A. A nude terracotta female figurine (mother goddess) from Period IV.
B. A votive tank, Period IV.
X. A Ringwell of Period IV.
B. Ringwell of Period IV.
XI. A. Copper coins of Period IV.
B. Copper coins of Period IV.
XII. A. Terracotta lids of Period IV.
B. Bottle-necked jars of Period IV.
XIII. A. Hearth from Period V.
B. Copper objects of Periods I & III.
XIV. A. Copper objects of Period III.
B. Copper and iron objects *in situ*, Period III.

XV. A. Copper bowl of Period III.
B. Miniature copper bowl of Period III.

XVI. A. Cooking vessel (*Hāndā*) of copper, Period III.
B. Cooking vessel (*Hāndā*) of copper, Period III.

XVII. A. Cooking vessel (*Hāndā*) of copper, Period III.
B. *Lota* of copper, Period III.

XVIII. A. Carinated *Hāndī* of copper, Period III.
B. Carinated *Hāndī* of copper, Period III.

XIX. A. Knobbed lid of copper, Period III.
B. Copper mirror, Period III.

XX. A. Iron swords, Period III.
B. Iron lampstand, Period III.

XXI. A. An ivory seal with legend 'Skandanaga' and its plaster cast, Period IV.
B. Sealing of baked clay with legend 'Harisenasya' and its reverse, Period IV.

XXII. A. Sealing of baked clay with legend 'Rudrapalasya' and with symbols,  and other sealings.
B. Beads of semi-precious stones, Periods I & II.

XXIII. A. Beads of semi-precious stones, Periods III & IV.
B. Beads of semi-precious stones, Periods IV & V.

XXIV. A. Terracotta beads of Periods I & II.
B. Terracotta beads of Periods III & IV.

XXV. A. Beads of faience, Period III.
B. Microphotograph of faience bead showing glassy phase, Period III.

XXVI. A. Microphotograph of faience bead showing angular quartz, Period III.
B. Microphotograph of faience bead, liquid silicate, Period III.

XXVII. A. Bone points and arrowheads, Periods I & II.
B. Bone points, Periods III & IV.

XXVIII. A. Bone points, Periods III & IV.
B. Antlers of Period II, III & IV.

XXIX. A. Pottery discs from Periods I, II & III.

	B.	Gamesmen from Periods I, II & III.
XXX.	A.	Skin rubbers, Period III.
	B.	Terracotta discs from Periods II & III.
XXXI.	A.	Terracotta human figurines, Period IV.
	B.	Terracotta human figurines, Period IV.
XXXII.	A.	Terracotta human figurines, Period IV.
	B.	Star-shaped figurines, Periods IV & V.
XXXIII.	A.	Terracotta animal figurines, Periods IV & V.
	B.	Terracotta animal figurines, Period V.

1

The Middle Ganga Plain

THE LAND

It is admitted that the Ganga has been cradle of Indian culture and civilization. As Sir Mortimer Wheeler said, 'if the Indus gave India a name, it may almost be said that the Ganges gave India a faith and is at least as worthy as her sister of our solicitude' (Wheeler, 1949 : 10). Dudley Stamp has noted that the plains of northern India form a great curve from the Arabian Sea to the Bay of Bengal. It is more than 3200 km long and 240 to 480 km broad. He writes that there are several outstanding features of this amazing area.

> One is the dead flatness of the plain—not a hill, scarcely a mound to break the monotony of the level surface.... So gentle is the seaward slope that it is imperceptible to the eye. Nearly a thousand miles from its mouth, the Ganga is only 900 feet above sea-level. Another feature is the sudden rise of the Himalayas from the level plain.... But otherwise the uniformity is amazing. Not a rock, not even a pebble is present, to alter the uniform character of the alluvium (Stamp, 1967 : 198-99).

The entire Ganga Plain is divided into three units : (i) The Upper Ganga Plain (ii) The Middle Ganga Plain (iii) The Lower Ganga Plain.

The Middle Ganga Plain stretches to about 300 km from the Himalayan foothills in the north and Vindhyan ranges in the south. It attained its present form during the Post-Tertiary period when this deep trough was filled up by fine alluvium brought down by the Himalayas with an average thickness of 1300-1400 metres. In prehistoric times, the main river Ganga, watered by several tributaries, flowed sluggishly in meandering fashion forming ox-bow lakes, some of which are perennial. These lakes were rich in aquatic fauna and the lands around them were covered with wild grasses, many of which had eatable grains. With the onset of milder climate of the Holocene, the marshy land gradually turned into good grassland which attracted small animals.

The basin expanded in the Middle Miocene and attained its present configuration in the Late Quaternary. Presently the Ganga Plain foreland basin is in a mature stage of evolution, with an oversupply of sediment and undefiled condition, building to 300-50 m above sea level, exclusively by fluvial processes (Singh, 1996: 99). The main rivers of the Ganga Plain, mainly the Ganga, Yamuna, Gomati, Ghaghara, etc., show very wide river valleys in which the present-day active channel · and its flood plain is intrenched. They are the areas of sand deposition in the Ganga Plain. The residence time of these main rivers in their valleys is on the order of 10^3-10^5 years during which several climatic and base-level changes have also transformed the character of the river channels and the nature of sediment (Singh, 1996: 129). The Ganga Plain is a peripheral foreland basin which came into existence in Early Miocene, expanded in the Middle Miocene and attained its present form in Late Quaternary. The stage-wise evolution took place in response to the thrust-fold belt loading events in the Himalayas and the consequent southward expansion of the basin (Singh, 1996: 133).

The Middle Ganga Plain is bounded by the Ganga-Yamuna confluence in the west and the West Bengal and Bihar border in the east, Himalayas in the north and the Vindhyas in the south. The area includes modern eastern Uttar Pradesh and parts of Bihar. On the basis of river system, the Middle Ganga Plain is further subdivided into (i) the Ganga Plain north and (ii) the Ganga Plain south, the former further subdivisible into (i) the Ganga-Ghaghara doab, (ii) The Ghaghara-Gandak interfluve, (iii) The Gandak-Kosi interfluve and the The Kosi-Mahananda interfluve. The Ganga Plain south is also further subdivisible into (a) the region to the west of Karmnasa (b) Karmnasa east interfluve, (c) Lower Son valley and (d) Magadha-Anga Plain. Needless to say, the Ganga remains the lifeline of the Middle Ganga Plain (Singh, 1971 : 190).

The Middle Ganga Plain, particularly its western section, is characterized by horseshoe lakes. Obviously these lakes were formed by the meander of shifting rivers. It is not unlikely that the river might have been the Ganga shifting towards south. At some places these horseshoe lake formations have been studied. The available evidence suggests that in the beginning there was very arid climatic condition followed by arid, semi-arid and semi-humid condition (Misra & Gupta, 1995 : 22).

Palynological studies of lake filled deposits in central Ganga Plain currently under progress, reveal that the Ganga Plain was mainly grassland at least for the last 15,000 years, with local forest thickets. Significantly, cultural pollens are present throughout the lake depositional history of last 15,000 years, suggesting anthropogenic activity in the region throughout this period. The cultural pollens in these profiles show changes with the changing climate history. For example, there is decrease in cultural pollens around 11, 500-10,500 yrs BP. There is increase in cultural pollen in last 5,000 years indicating advanced anthropogenic activity (Tewari *et al.*, 2003).

THE DRAINAGE SYSTEM

The drainage system of Middle Ganga Plain is governed by the general life of the land which slopes from the north-west to the south-east. The entire region is drained by the Ganga system. Most of the left-hand tributaries of the Ganga have their sources in the Himalayas and are thus perennial. The right-hand tributaries rise in the plateau and are seasonal. Most of these have only a narrow ribbon of water straggling through the vast span of sands in summer and winter.

The Ganga system can be further subdivided into five sub-systems :

1. The Ghaghara System
2. The Gandak System
3. The Kosi System
4. The Son System
5. The Remaining Tributaries

The Ganga System

The Ganga has its catchment area in the snowy Himalaya and flows with the gradiant of 9.5 c, per km from west to east. The right bank of the river is generally steep and 8-15 m high during dry months. The left bank is generally flat and low, but at places where it has formed hard gravel exposure, rises even 10-12 m high from the river bed during dry months (Singh, 1973; 13).

The Ghaghara System

This system consists of four main river, i.e. the Ghaghara and its three main left-hand tributaries—the Kuwana, the Rapti and the little Gandak which in their turn receive numerous tributaries. The Ghaghara rises in the snowy Himalayas and has a gradiant of 12 cm per km. The Rapti rises in the Nepal Himalayas and the little Gandak and the left-hand tributaries of Rapti like Burhi Rapti, Banganga, Ghonghi, Rohin, etc. take their rise in the Shivalik foothills; others like Ami, Kuwana, Manwar, etc., originate from the *tals* of the plain. All the rivers of this system are notorious for dangerous floods. The Ghaghara and the Rapti flow in frequently changing courses caused by constraint erosion and a deposition on a large scale.

The Gandak System

While the Ghaghara system has many tributaries, the Gandak does not have any important tributary to it. Instead, there are a number of its own old beds, distributaries and spill channels. The Gandak is formed by the confluence of seven streams (Saptgandaki) and has a higher gradient (18 cm per km) than the Ganga or the Ghaghara. Its ever changing courses and the disasterous flood play havock in the area and prove more disasterous than those of the Ghaghara system.

The Kosi System

The main river of this system is the Kosi which is formed by the confluence of seven important streams originating in eastern Nepal. The principal branch, the Sun Kosi, running west to east, is joined by other 6 rivers, i.e. the Bhotia Kosi, the Tamba Kosi, the Likhu Kosi, the Dudh Kosi, the Arun Kosi and the Tamber Kosi. It enters in the Indian territory near Bagia Ghat and joins the Ganga a little below Karagola.

The Kosi has various radiating distributaries system like Saura, Barhandi, Dhusan, Tilaleh and its tributaries like Sugarus, Balan, Kamla, etc. This river has a larger catchment area with an average gradient of about 24 cm per km. The Kosi floods and the deposition of micaceous sands have caused colossal damage which has earned it the epithet of 'The Sorrow of Bihar'.

The Son System

The Son is the only river of this system without any tributary. It has a broad, shallow, red sandy bed which at places attains a breadth of about 3.2 km. During the rains it flows with considerable amount of water but in the dry months the bed presents a wide stretch of drifting sand with an insignificant stream of water.

The Remaining Tributaries

Apart from the main tributaries discussed above separately, the left-hand tributaries of Ganga from Allahabad to Hajipur are the Baruna, the Gomati, the Gangi, the Besu, the Mangai, the Chhoti Saryu (Tons in the upper reaches), the Mahi, etc. They rise in the plains and flow almost parallel to each other from north-west to south-east. They attain formidable sizes during the rains but in the dry months they are fordable. Among its right-hand tributaries west of the Son, the important ones are the Tons and Karmnasa, which are seasonal in nature and are flooded for a very short period (Singh, 1973 : 13).

THE FLORA

The annual average rainfall of the area is about 1000 mm. The natural vegetation cover has now been completely obliterated on account of increasing population pressure and consequent human manipulation. However, remains of typical tropical dry deciduous woodland can be seen in heavily degraded and isolated patches in the area. As indicated by pollen analysis (Gupta, 1976, Pant & Pant, 1980), in the past the area was covered with grassy vegetation. The small shrubs and trees which still survive in the bad land ravines include dhak (*Butea menosperma)*, sheesham (*Dalbergia sissoo*), siras (*Albizzia lebbck*), banyan (*Ficus glomerata*), pakar (*Ficus infectorisa*), pipal (*Ficus religiosa*), mahua (*Basia latifolia*), tamarind (*Tamurindus indica*), neem (*Azadirachta indica*), babul (*Acacia arabica*), kaitha (*Feronia elephantum*), chilbil (*Ulmus* integrifolicus), lisora (*Cordia myxa*), etc. (Pal, 2002: 61).

Traces of earliest human activity have been found in the hilly tract of the Vindhyas and the colonization of Middle Ganga Plain is comparatively late in point of time. Lower Paleolithic tools were documented on top terraces of the rivers and hillocks jutting out of the main hills where a finer variety of quartzite is available as rubble. On most of the hillocks south of the Belan such as Murli Mahugarh, Chandatari, Ramgarh, Belrahi, etc., Lower Palaeolithic sites have been located and a large number of tools have been collected (Varma, 1999 : 178). The Lower Palaeolithic in the Vindhyan region was succeeded by the Middle Palaeolithic industries of blade-flake-scraper tradition. Besides the river valleys, the Middle Palaeolithic sites are located on the slopes of hills and very low hillocks under the shelter of high hills and on the terraces of the rivers. Among the Middle Palaeolithic sites of the Vindhyan region, mention may be made of Bataubir, Khutabir, Marwa, Naunkalan, south of the Belan valley and Patpara in the middle Son valley. Stone tools in this culture are made of fine-grained quartzite and comprise mainly scrapers, blades, points and borers. Among them scrapers of different types outnumber all the other type of tools. A large number of animal fossils associated with this culture have been collected from the Belan valley. They include *Bos gaurus, Bovidae spp., Cervidae sp., Sus.* Hippo, *Equus sp.,* Rhino, *Elephas,* etc.

Lithic and bone artefacts, chronologically assignable to the Middle Palaeolithic have been recorded from the Kalpi section in the Yamuna valley. These artefacts have been recovered from a straitigraphically constrained sediment horizon dated by Infrared Stimulated Luminescence (IRSL) technique to around 45,000 years BC. The lithic artefacts are made mostly on 2-4 cm size quartzite pebbles. The type includes atypical points, side scrapers and chips and occur in limited area. The bone artefacts far exceed in number over the lithic artefacts. The bone artefacts are end-scraper, point, notched tool, burin, atypical, end scraper and bones with cut marks (Tewari, *et al.,* 2002: in press).

CULTURE-SEQUENCE

Epi-Palaeolithic

The Epi-Palaeolithic or late Upper Palaeolithic constitutes an important stage in the prehistory of the Vindhyas. It is represented by parallel sided blades, blunted back blades, scrapers, points, burins and borers along with cores, flakes and debetage which are made of cherty material. These are comparatively large in size and in technique, typology and raw material compare well with the Epi-Palaeolithic assemblages of the Belan and Son valleys. Remains of Epi-Palaeolithic have been identified on Kurha, Gharwa, Suleman Parvatpur, Salhipur, Mandah and other sites.

For computing the chronology of Epi-Palaeolithic-Mesolithic culture of the Middle Ganga Valley, it may be noted that these people had come in the Ganga Plain from the Vindhyan area. Radiocarbon dates have been obtained from the Upper Palaeolithic and Epi-Palaeolithic horizons of the Belan valley. Gravel III, the Upper Palaeolithic horizon in the Belan valley, has yielded two dates reading 17785 ± 330 BC and 23870 ± 810-730 BC. Five dates have been obtained from Gravel IV at Mahagara. These dates read 8080 ± 115 BC, 8175 ± 160 BC, 9360 ± 190 BC, 9945 ± 180 BC and 12200 ± 400 BC. In the light of the above the Epi-Palaeolithic phase of the Middle Ganga Valley may be dated provisionally between 17,000 BC and 10,000 BC (Misra & Gupta, 1995 : 30).

Mesolithic

Intensive excavations conducted by the universities of Allahabad and Banaras during the 1960s and 1970s resulted in the discovery of more than 500 Mesolithic sites—mainly in the eastern Vindhyas and the Middle Ganga Valley. In the Vindhyas Mesolithic sites lie in the district of Sidhi, Satna and Rewa in Madhya Pradesh and Banda, Allahabad, Mirzapur,

Sonbhadra and the hilly parts of Chandauli in eastern Uttar Pradesh. In the Middle Ganga Valley the Mesolithic sites are located in parts of Allahabad, Varanasi, Pratapgarh, Jaunpur and Sultanpur districts (Misra, 1997: 32). Of the 500 sites listed above, nearly 200 sites are located in the Middle Ganga Valley. This increase in the number of Mesolithic sites is an indication of the fact that there was a spurt in the population. This could have been due to a number of factors such as large-scale migration and intermingling of people, moderate climate, easy availability of food due to the development of a more efficient hunting kit and trapping techniques (Varma, 1999: 184).

Of these, 13 Mesolithic sites were excavated by the University of Allahabad. Among the excavated sites Morhana Pahar, Chopani Mando, Baghor II, Madhauli, Banki, Ghagharia and Dhanuhi are located in the Vindhyas and the remaining three—Sarai Nahar Rai, Mahadaha and Damdama—are situated in Pratapgarh district. Besides these, Lahariadih, situated in the Sonbhadra district was excavated by the Banaras Hindu University. These investigations have yielded valuable information about the Mesolithic culture.

As the flat Ganga Plain did not provide the Mesolithic man with natural shelters, he made small huts, circular or oval, supported by bamboo poles. House plans of 20 circular or oval huts were exposed at Chopani Mando and similar evidence comes from Sarai Nahar Rai and Damdama. Rammed and plastered floors were exposed at the latter site. The people cooked their food in circular or oval pits. Small hearths were recognised at Chopani Mando, Sarai Nahar Rai and Damdama. A community hearth was also exposed at Damdama. These hearths have yielded burnt clay lumps, charred and semi-charred animal bones along with loose blackish soil. This shows that animal flesh, birds, tortoise and fish, etc., were roasted in these hearths. An interesting feature of the Ganga Valley sites is that numerous animal bones have been found. The animal species identified include *bos gaurus*, sheep/goat, cow, stag, deer, rhinoceros, elephant, etc. (Thomas *et al.*, 1995; Thomas *et al.*, 1996). No domestication is indicated at these sites. Other animal bones are found in charred condition suggesting thereby that these were hunted and consumed by the Mesolithic people.

As it is too well known, microlithic tools are the hallmark of the Mesolithic tool technology. Thus, tools were fashioned on blades through the punch technique during this period. Blades were converted into parallel sided blades, backed blades, pen-knives, lunates, triangles, trapezes, tanged points, side-scrapers and end-scrapers, burins, etc. However, since no lithic raw material is available in the Ganga Valley, the inhabitants developed alternative strategies to cope with this problem. Firstly, utmost economy was practised by reducing the length, breadth and thickness of the microliths. Residual cores are almost absent on the Ganga Valley sites. By adopting this method they could draw out large number of microlithic flakes/ blades from a single core. Secondly, bone tool technology was developed as an alternative to lithic tools. The percentage of bone tools in relation to lithic tools increases as we proceed from lower levels to upper levels. It is interesting to note that bone tools are almost absent in the Vindhyan sites (Varma, 1999: 186).

The excavations have also yielded food processing implements—querns, mullers, hammers, stone sharpeners, etc., made in sandstone, quartzite or basalt. The occurrence of these objects at Mesolithic sites indicates that the people collected wild cereals and edible roots for supplementing their diet. In this context the occurrence of wild rice from the late Mesolithic phase at Chopani Mando assumes considerable importance.

Another interesting feature of Mesolithic culture of Ganga Valley is the discovery of a large number of burials which provide considerable evidence regarding the funerary customs and eschatological beliefs of the Mesolithic people. A fairly good number of burials have been excavated from Sarai Nahar Rai, Mahadaha and at Damdama. At Sarai Nahar Rai, 11 graves were opened. From 10 graves skeletal remains of single individuals were found while in one, 4 individuals were buried together at the same time. At Mahadaha as many as 30 skeletons were exposed. Here there were atleast two cases of double burials. At Damdama 41 graves were exposed. Of these, 35 graves yielded skeletal remains of single individuals. In 5 graves double burials were encountered while 1 grave yielded skeletal remains of 3 individuals. Of the double burials, in four cases the skeletal remains were those of male and female while in 1 grave both the skeletons appear to be those of males. The triple burial at the site yielded skeletal remains of 2 males and 1 female (Misra, 1997a: 35).However, all these burials were made in a set pattern. The meticulous way in which the graves were prepared and the way the skeletons lie, represents the performance of a ritual at a group level. The graves were oblong and shallow. The width was increased in case the grave was meant to receive more than one body. The excavation of burials at Damdama suggests that some sort of a fire ritual was performed in the grave itself just before burying the dead (Varma, 1999: 187). Generally the bodies were placed west-east with the head towards the west. But some graves with east-west orientation were also found. There is an exception in which a couple has been buried in north-south and south-north orientation. The bodies have generally been buried in an extended position on their back. In one case the body has been buried in supine position. Funerary offerings in the form of microliths, bones, fresh water molluscs and antler ornaments not only confirm that the people believed in life beyond death but had also developed elaborate ritual practices. Taking into account the number of querns and muller as variables, an attempt has been made to make an estimate of the population of these Mesolithic sites. In traditional rural India, a family unit normally has one set of grinding stones and if we use this model for the prehistoric period, we can extrapolate a population estimate. During the last phase of Mahadaha, 191 and at Damdama 110 querns were recovered. If we assume a minimum of four to five persons per unit, the population at Mahadaha would work out to between 700 to 1000 and at Damdama from 550 to 650. Considering the size of the habitation site, this does not seem to be a wild guess (Varma, 1999 : 187).

An examination of skeletal remains obtained from the three excavated sites by biological anthropologists shows that the Mesolithic man was impressive in appearance—well-built, muscular, tall and hyper robust who had attained his full ontogenetic potential in a demanding hunting-foraging lifestyle (Misra, 2002; 21). There are 15 well-preserved skeletons in the Sarai Nahar Rai series. Of the 10 skeletons examined by Kennedy, 7 are males and 3 are females. All are adults with age range for males being 16 to 24 years, for females being 15 to 35 years. These ranges of death age are close to values obtained from other Mesolithic population in South Asia and Eurasia (Misra, 2002 : 21).

Mahadaha had yielded 32 skeletons in 28 graves. These include 17 males, 7 females, 1 adult of uncertain sex and 3 children. Age range is 18 to 40 years for males and 30 to 65 years for females, young and adult from 18 to 34 years predominating for both sexes. Like the Sarai Nahar Rai people, the Mahadahans were also tall and they exhibit large and robust post cranial bones.The third excavated site, Damdama, has yielded 47 skeletons from 41 graves. Lukacs and his associates (Lukacs *et al.*, 1996) who studied these skeletons, determined that 50 per cent of these were males, 40 per cent females and 9 were of undetermined sex (Misra, 2002: 25).

The chronology of Mesolithic culture of the Middle Ganga Valley is based on three radiocarbon dates obtained from Sarai Nahar Rai, Damdama and Paisara. The date from Sarai Nahar Rai reads 8395 ± 110 BC. A TL date from Damdama falls between 7000 and 5000 BC. The radiocarbon date from Mesolithic level at Paisara reads 7420 ± 110 BC. Similar dates come from Baghor II and other sites. On the basis of combined testimony of these sites the beginning of Mesolithic culture in the Middle Ganga Valley may be placed between 10,000 BC and 5000 BC (Misra & Gupta, 1995: 31).

Neolithic

The succeeding stage of human evolution is termed as Neolithic. This stage was marked by the breeding of wild animals and cultivation of selected wild grasses. The first animals to be domesticated were dog, cattle, sheep and goat and the first plants to be cultivated were rice, wheat and barley. This change occurred around ten thousand years ago or even earlier in the vast stretch of mountainous and hilly environment extending from the east coast of the Mediterranean to the eastern edge of Baluchistan plateau as also in the Yangtze valley in China (Yasuda, 2002). In India, evidence of Neolithic culture have been found in north-western India, Kashmir,Vindhyan region, Middle Ganga Valley, south-eastern India, north-eastern India and southern India. The Neolithic cultures of these regions are characterized by sedentary settlements, cultivation of cereal plants, domestication of selected animals, ground stone industries including a microlithic component, handmade pottery, etc. In the Middle Ganga Valley evidence of Neolithic settlements comes from Lahuradeva (district Sant Kabir Nagar), Sohgaura and Imlidih Khurd in district Gorakhpur of Uttar Pradesh and Chirand, Chechar-Kutubpur, Taradih and Senuwar in Bihar. The excavations, though conducted on a limited scale have brought to light the evidence of wattle-and-daub structures. Traces of post-holes have been noticed. Screen walls of huts were made of split bamboo reeds, the impression of which have been found in the burnt clay lumps. The hutments appear to be round or oval on plan. At Chirand, evidence of pit dwelling has also been reported.

The excavations have yielded rich data regarding the ceramics used by the Neolithic folks of the Ganga Valley. In the early stages they used to make handmade pottery but the use of wheel-turned pot has also been reported from some of the Neolithic sites (Senuwar) from the upper strata of this culture. Corded ware appears to be characteristic trait of the Neolithic culture, both of the Vindhyas and the Middle Ganga Valley. Other ceramic industries comprise ordinary red ware, burnished ware, rusticated ware, Black-and-Red Ware, lustrous ware and lustrous red ware. The principal types are bowls with varying profiles, vases, squatted vessels and miniature jars. The clay used for pottery contains gritty, rice husk and chaff as degraissant. A limited number of painted sherds have also been reported from Chirand and Senuwar. These post-firing paintings, confined to the rim have been executed in red ochre. At Chirand the painted motifs include linear design of criss-cross lines and concentric circles. This diversity of ceramic industries and types strongly suggests that the potter had acquired sufficient technical skill in ceramic tradition.

The stone objects of Neolithic culture comprise flakes, blades, scrapers, arrowheads, points, lunates and borers made on cilicious stones like chert, chalcedony, agate, jasper, quartz, etc. Rounded celts of basalt and granite have been found at Chirand and Senuwar. Bone objects constitute another trait of the Neolithic culture of the Middle Ganga Valley. They include celts, scrapers, stylli and arrowheads. Excavations at Chirand have yielded plenty of such objects. In this context, it may be noted that with the exception of the Neolithic sites of the Kashmir valley, Chirand is the only Neolithic site in India to produce bone objects, both in quality and variety (Misra & Gupta, 1995 : 26). Terracotta objects from the Neolithic sites in the Middle Ganga Valley are not many but Chirand had yielded terracotta wheels, beads, bangles, cakes, birds, serpents, etc.

As stated above, the domestication of animals and cultivation of cereal plants are the hallmark of the Neolithic culture. The Neolithic people of the Middle Ganga Valley also cultivated wheat, barley, rice, field pea, lentil, *masur, moong,* etc. The evidence from Senuwar and Chirand is copious. Rice appears to be the staple food of the Neolithic people. Evidence of cultivated rice along with its wild progenitor has been recently found embedded in the core of a number of potsherds from Lahuradeva from Period IA. The two radiocarbon dates obtained from this level have been dated to 5298 ± 160 and 4196 ± 90 BC (BS-1966 and BS-1951) (Tewari *et al.*, 2002 : 54-62). Thus the cultivation of rice now goes back to the late 6th and 5th millennium BC in the Sarayupar region of the Middle Ganga Valley. Bones of cattle, buffalo, elephant, rhinoceros, stag and deer have been found from these sites. Of these, cattle and buffalo were domesticated while stag and deer were obviously hunted. As rhinoceros has never been domesticated, during the Neolithic phase also it would have roamed wild in the marshy areas of the Middle Ganga Valley (Misra & Gupta, 1995 : 27).

For fixing the chronology of Neolithic culture of the Middle Ganga Valley, the dates from Chirand and Senuwar may be taken into consideration. Two radiocarbon dates reading 1760 ± 150 BC and 1680 ± 135 BC push back the beginning the Neolithic culture around 2000 BC at Chirand. The overlap phase of the Neolithic-Chalcolithic levels at Senuwar has provided four radiocarbon dates. All these dates taken together, push back the beginning of the Neolithic culture earlier than 2000 BC. The newly obtained dates from Lahuradeva place this culture around 5000 BC but this needs to be supported by more data.

CHALCOLITHIC

The Neolithic period was succeeded by the Chalcolithic. The general pattern of life did not change during this period, barring some significant developments. The introduction of metals (copper/ bronze), though limited in quantity, had a profound effect on the quality of life. However, as the supply of metal was very limited, stone tools continued to be used side by side and hence this stage of human evolution has been aptly termed as Chalcolithic. This stage witnessed a marked increase in the number of settlements, introduction of copper-bronze for the manufacture of tools, weapons and ornaments, improvement in architecture, introduction of wheel-made pottery and diversification of wares and profuse decoration of vessels by painted, incised and applique designs (Misra, 2001: 512). A number of Chalcolithic sites have been found in different parts of the country and the Middle Ganga Plain is no exception. Some of the important Chalcolithic sites of this region are listed below:

Pure Deojani, Pelkhawar and Bhelwani in Pratapgarh, Akahua in Jaunpur, Rajghat, Prahladpur, Sarai-Mohana and Kamauli in Varanasi; Mason Dih in Ghazipur, Nahusa Raja Ka Tila in Mau; Banwarighat, Gularihwaghat, Susipar, Ramnagarghat, Baragaon and Gerar in Basti, Lahuradeva in Sant Kabir Nagar; Khairadih, Waina and Bhunadih in Ballia, Sohgaura, Narhan, Dhuriapar and Imlidih Khurd in Gorakhpur; Purainadih in Maharajganj; Malhar, Raja-Nala-Ka-Tila in Sonbhadra; Jhusi in Allahabad district of Uttar Pradesh and Chirand and Manjhi in Saran; Maner in Patna; Oriup and Champa in Bhagalpur; Chechar-Kutubpur in Vaisali; Sonpur and Taradih in Gaya and Senuwar in Rohtas district in Bihar. Out of these, Rajghat, Prahladpur, Sarai-Mohana, Kamauli, Masondih, Sohgaura, Narhan, Dhuriapar, Imlidih Khurd, Waina, Bhunadih, Khairadih, Lahuradeva, Jhusi, Malhar, Raja-Nala-Ka-Tila, Chirand, Manjhi, Maner, Oriup, Champa, Chechar-Kutubpur, Sonpur, Taradih and Senuwar have been excavated.

Most of these sites are located on river banks, big or small, or on horseshoe lakes. The size of settlements ranges from small to medium. In the absence of large-scale excavations at any of these sites, no definite statement can be made regarding the planning of the settlement. However, the occurrence of burnt clay lumps with split bamboo or reed impressions at a number of sites shows that the Chalcolithic people constructed the walls with this material. The walls were plastered with mud on both sides (Misra & Gupta, 1995 : 27). Evidence of post-holes comes from a number of sites including Imlidih Khurd which indicates that the construction of huts was circular or oval on plan. Plastered floors and various types of hearths have been excavated at a number of sites including Narhan, Imlidih Khurd and Waina. The principal ceramic industry of the Chalcolithic culture of Mid Ganga Valley is the white painted Black-and-Red Ware which constitutes as much as 58 per cent of the ceramic range at Narhan.

The other associated wares are the black slipped ware, the red slipped ware and red ware in sizeable quantity and grey ware in limited quantity. Bowls of various types (shallow, straight or convex-sided, carinated, lipped and channel, etc.), convex sided bowl-cum-lid and platters are common types. Convex-sided dishes have also been reported from some sites but this type is totally absent on sites of Sarayupar plain. Elongated beakers with external grooves at the waist, button-based goblets and pedestal bowls are important shapes in the black slipped ware. Tumbler or *lota* which is a hallmark of the present-day kitchen of almost all the North Indian villages is present on sites of Ballia district (Waina, Bhunadih, etc.) and another characteristic type, open mouth jar or *martban* also is a speciality of the same region. Cooking vessels or *hāndīs* with short concave or carinated neck and with applique designs on the exterior are present in red ware at Imlidih Khurd. Miniature and small vase and dish-on-stand are also present in limited number. Spouted vessels in red ware are a characteristic feature of Chalcolithic culture of the Sarayupar plain.

The painted designs are present in Black-and-Red Ware but they occur on limited sherds of black slipped ware and red ware. The painted designs are mostly geometric (linear) and occur on both sides of the vessel. Besides painting, the pottery of Sarayupar plain also exhibits other decorations in the form of cut, incised, applique, knobbed and corded designs. Corded designs are present in Period I at Imlidih Khurd and in lower levels at Lahuradeva which has a Neolithic affiliation; but they continue to survive in the transitional phase from the Neolithic to Chalcolithic at this site. A few sherds with post-firing scratched designs comprising mostly geometric motifs were reported from Imlidih Khurd and it was a pleasant surprise to see the same patterns on the red ware obtained from Lahuradeva where excavation is currently under progress.

Microliths are an essential component of the Chalcolithic sites of the Vindhyas and some sites of the Middle Ganga Valley such as Sringaverapura, Prahladpur, Waina, Chirand, Taradih and Senuwar. Non-availability of raw material was most probably the compelling factor for the restricted use of the lithic tools in the Ganga Valley and its total absence in the Sarayupar plain (Narhan and other sites). The microlithic tools comprise various types of blades, points, arrowheads, scrapers, lunates, triangles and trapezes together with a large number of cores. The tools are fashioned on semi-precious stones—chalcedony, chert and occasionally, carnelian, agate and quartz. A few sites have also yielded polished celts (Narhan) and chisels of basalt. Obviously, they are survival of the preceding Neolithic culture. The Chalcolithic people used different type of ornaments (beads, pendants, bangles, rings, ear-stud, etc.). The beads are generally made on semi-precious stones and occasionally on bone, shell, faience, steatite, copper, gold and conch. Among the other objects recovered from various sites, mention may be made of saddle querns, mullers, rubbers and hammerstones—all made of stone. Fish-hook, pin, needle, stylus, etc., made of bone and terracotta, hopscotch, stopper and gamesmen complete the artifectual inventory of the Chalcolithic people.

As stated earlier, the technology of Chalcolithic people comprized mainly of tools and weapons of copper and stone but also bone and antler. The copper objects, though limited in number, comprise knives, spearheads and arrowheads. Bone and antler tools comprise awls, points, tanged arrowheads and barbed arrowheads with socketed base. Microliths and blade tools have been found at almost all the sites but they are absent in the Sarayupar plain.

The economy of the people as obtained from several sites of the Middle Ganga Valley was based on cultivation, domestication, hunting and gathering. Cultivated plants include wheat, barley, rice, *jowar*, *moong*, gram, *kodon* (a coarse millet grown only in tropical countries), lentil, *til* (sesame), linseed and pea.

A good quantity of archaeo-botanical remains obtained by flotation from Narhan give a fair idea of the agricultural practices of the Chalcolithic people of the Sarayupar plain. Grains of hulled and 6-row barley (*Hordeum vulgare*), club wheat (*T. compactum*), bread wheat (*T. aestivum*), dwarf wheat (*T. sphaeorococcum*) and cultivated rice (*Oryza sativa*) have been identified. The pulses include pea (*Pisum sativum*), green gram (*moong*: *Vigna radiata*), gram/chick pea (*C icer arietinum*), *Khesari* (*Lathyrus sativus*), besides mustard oilseeds and flask/linseed. Seeds of jack fruit (*Artocarpos integrifolious*) found from these levels is an important discovery. Jack fruit grows wild in the western ghats and it was taken for cultivation to North India. The present evidence suggests that the Narhan inhabitants cultivated it for its fruit (Saraswat in Singh, 1994).

Domesticated animals include buffalo, sheep/goat, pig and dog and wild animals include several species of deer, antelope and boar. Remains of birds and acquatic creatures like fish and tortoise have also been found from several sites.

For the chronology of the Chalcolithic culture of this region, the dates obtained from Sohgaura, Narhan, Khairadih, Chirand and Senuwar may be taken into account. There are five radiocarbon dates each from Senuwar and Chirand while Khairadih has yielded three dates. Sohgaura and Narhan have given two radiocarbon dates each. The combined testimony of all these dates places the Chalcolithic culture of the Middle Ganga Valley in a time bracket of 1500 BC-900 BC. However, the recent radiocarbon dates from Lahuradeva put the beginning of the Chalcolithic culture around 2000 BC.

IRON AGE

The succeeding culture in the Mid Ganga Plain belongs to the Early Iron Age. Vestiges of this culture have been found on almost in all the sites noted above and there is no stratigraphic break between the Chalcolithic and the Early Iron Age assemblage. An interesting development is some early radiocarbon dates from Raja-Nala-Ka-Tila, Malhar and Jhusi which put the introduction of the Early Iron Age to the mid second millennium BC. These dates are tabulated below for the benefit of readers.

TABLE 1.1 RADIOCARBON AGES OF RAJA-NALA-KA-TILA

Sl. No.	*Laboratory No.*	*Layer/Depth*	*Radiocarbon age in years BP/BC 5568 ± 110 BP*	*Calibrated age based on half life 5530 ± 40 years*	*One Sigma*
1.	BS-1378 1996-97 Trench No. U-19	(6) 1.95-2.00 m With Iron	2550 ± 110 BP 600 ± 110 BC	2626 ± 110 BP 676 ± 110 BC	822 (773) 486 BC
2.	PRL-2047 1996-97 Trench No. U-20	(6) 2.08-2.10 m With Iron	2890 ± 90 B 940 ± 90 BC	2980 ± 90 BP 1130 ± 90 BC	1196 BC—1188 BC 1164 BC—1143 BC 1132 BC—976 BC 970 BC—930 BC
3.	BS-1299 1995-96 Trench No. A-1	Pit Sealed by layer (6) With iron	2830 ± 100 BP 880 ± 100 BC	2914 ± 100 BP 960 ± 100 BC	1118 (963) 859 BC
4.	BS-1300 1995-96 Trench No. A-1	(6) 2.00 m With iron	3090 ± 110 BP 1110 ± 110 BC	3150 ± 110 BP 1200 ± 110 BC	1423 (1307) 1144 BC

Cont. Table 1.1

Table 1.1 Cont.

Sl. No.	*Laboratory No.*	*Layer/Depth*	*Radiocarbon age in years BP/BC 5568 ± 110 BP*	*Calibrated age based on half life 5530 ± 40 years*	*One Sigma*
5.	PRL-2049 1996-97 Trench No. T-19	(7) 2.40-2.45 With iron	3050 ± 90 BP 1100 ± 90 BC	3150 ± 90 BP 1200 ± 90 BC	1406 BC—1198 BC 1186 BC—1164 BC 1143 BC—1132 BC
6.	PRL-2046 1996-97 Trench No. U-19	(9) 2.80 m Without iron	3100 ± 90 BP 1150 ± 90 BC	3200 ± 90 BP 1250 ± 90 BC	1500 BC—1490 BC 1448 BC—1256 BC 1240-BC—1214 BC
7.	PRL-2045 1996-97 Trench No. U-20	(10) 2.90 m Without iron	3260 ± 90 BP 1310 ± 90 BC	3360 ± 90 BP 1410 ± 90 BC	1622 BC—1426 BC 1742 BC—1378 BC 1348 BC—1316 BC

TABLE 1.2 RADIOCARBON AGES OF MALHAR

Sl. No.	*Laboratory No.*	*Radiocarbon ages in BP/BC on the basis of half life*		*Cal BC Stuiver et al. One Sigma*
		5568 ± 30 years	*5730 ± 40 years*	
1.	BS-1623, MLR II Trench No. XA1 Layer No. (3) Depth 0.55 cm	3450 ± 90 BP 1500 ± 90 BC	3550 ± 90 BP 1600 ± 90 BC	1882 (1743) 1639 BC
2.	BS-1614, MLR II Trench No.A1 Pit sealed by Layer No. (3) Depth 61-63 cm	6380 ± 110 BP 4330 ± 110 BC. 5262 BC	6570 ± 110 BP 4620 ± 110 BC	5475 (5368, 5351, 5340, 5329, 5323

Cont. Table 1.2

Table 1.2 Cont.

Sl. No.	*Laboratory No.*	*Radiocarbon ages in BP/BC on the basis of half life*		*Cal BC Stuiver et al. One Sigma*
		5568 ± 30 years	*5730 ± 40 years*	
3.	BS-1593, MLR II Trench No. A1 Pit sealed by Layer No. (3) Depth 90-100 cm	3540 ± 90 BP 1590 ± 90 BC	3650 ± 90 BP 1700 ± 90 BC	2012 (1882, 1836 1834) 1742 BC
4.	BS-1590, MLR II Trench No. XA1 Layer No. (4) Depth 0.80 cm	3740 ± 80 BP 1790 ± 80 BC	3850 ± 80 BP 1900 ± 80 BC	2283 (2141) 1984 BC

TABLE 1.3 RADIOCARBON DATES OF JHUSI

Sl. No.	Trench details	Radiocarbon yrs BC		Date in BC/AD	Calibrated dates in BC/AD
		5568 ± 30	5730 ± 40		
AU/JHS/1 2068	C/12 (15) 510	Kushan 1850 ± 80	1910 ± 90	40 ± 90 AD	(133) 316 AD 74
AU/JHS/3 2070	C/14 (30) 555	Late NBPW 2140 ± 90	2200 ± 90	250 ± 90 BC	357 (195) (195, 173) 46 BC
AU/JHS63 413)	C/15 (37) 1025	Mid NBPW 2430 ± 90	2500 ± 90	550 ± 90 BC	763 (498, 2070 393 BC
AU/JHS/8 2074	C/15 (43) 1165	Early NBPW 2520 ± 90	2590 ± 90	640 ± 90 BC	799(763, 676, 674) 393 BC
AU/JHS/9 2075	C/15 (46) 1210	Pre NBPW 2650 ± 90 with iron	2730 ± 90	780 ± 90 BC	897 (806) 789 BC
AU/JHS/ 12 2077	C/15 (49) 1240	Pre NBPW 2820 ± 90 with iron	2900 ± 90	950 ± 90 BC	1107 (973 956, 941) 844 BC

Cont. Table 1.3

Table 1.3 Cont.

Sl. No.	Trench details	Radiocarbon yrs BC		Date in BC/AD	Calibrated dates in BC/AD
		5568 ± 30	5730 ± 40		
AU/JHS/ 16 2081	C/15 (53) 1325	Pre-iron 2700 ± 90 (Chalcolithic)	2780 ± 90	830 ± 90 BC	966 (830) 799 BC
AU/JHS/ 18 2083	C/15 (62) 1520	Pre-iron 3200 ± 90 (Chalcolithic)	3290 ± 90	1340 ± 90 BC	1597 (1490, 1480, 1450) 1400 BC

2

Results of Agiabir Excavations

Archaeological investigations carried out in the Sarayupar plain by the present team had resulted into the documentation of a new protohistoric culture termed as **Narhan Culture** (Singh, 1994). This pre-iron culture with white painted Black-and-Red Ware as the principal ceramic industry flourished in the second half of the second millennium BC. Vestiges of Narhan culture have been found, besides the type-site, at Imlidih Khurd, Dhuriapar (both in district Gorakhpur), Bhunadih, Waina and Khairadih (all in district Ballia) on the Ghaghara and its tributaries (Singh, 1996). Recently some new dimensions have been added to this culture by excavations at Raja-Nala-Ka-Tila in district Sonbhadra (Tewari, 1997 : 77-95) as also at Malhar, district Chandauli (Tewari, 1998 : 57-67) (Fig. 1). However, on all these sites this culture has been noticed on small settlements (mostly village sites not exceeding two hectares in size) and a transition from primitive to complex society represented by urban centres like Kausambi, Sravasti and Rajghat could not be securely documented. Therefore in order to understand this transition, an urban settlement having continuous habitation from Narhan culture to the early medieval period needed to be investigated. Agiabir perfectly fitted this bill as the settlement is spread over an area of more than 40 acres along the Ganga and it has provided an uninterrupted sequence of cultures from second millennium BC (Narhan culture) to the end of the Gupta period. This site was explored by the second author in June, 1998 (Singh, 1999 : 51-56). With the above objective in mind, the present team conducted excavations at this site for three field seasons (from 1999 and 2001) and a summary account of this investigation is given subsequently.

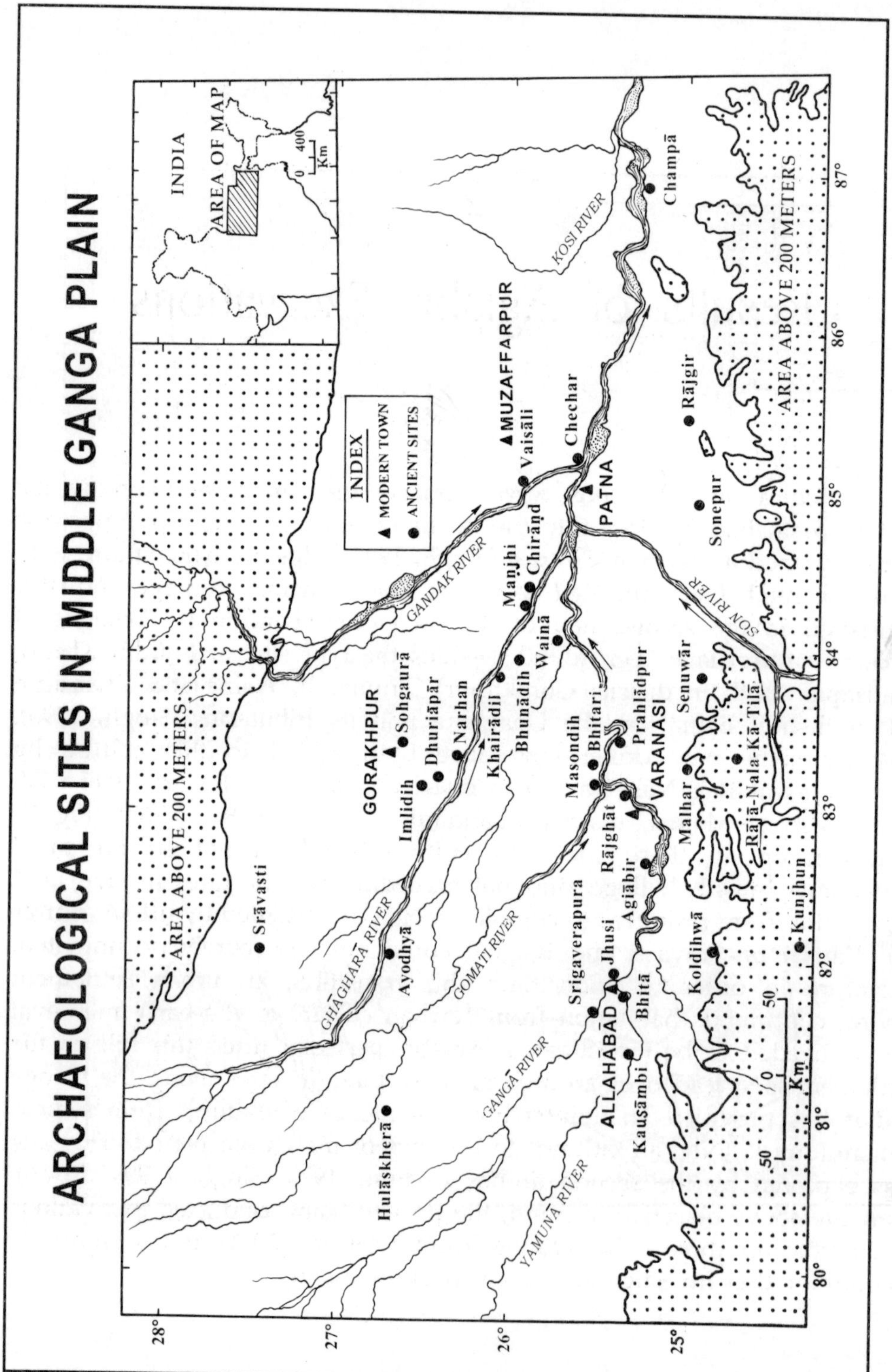

Fig. 1. Archaeological sites in the Middle Ganga Plain.

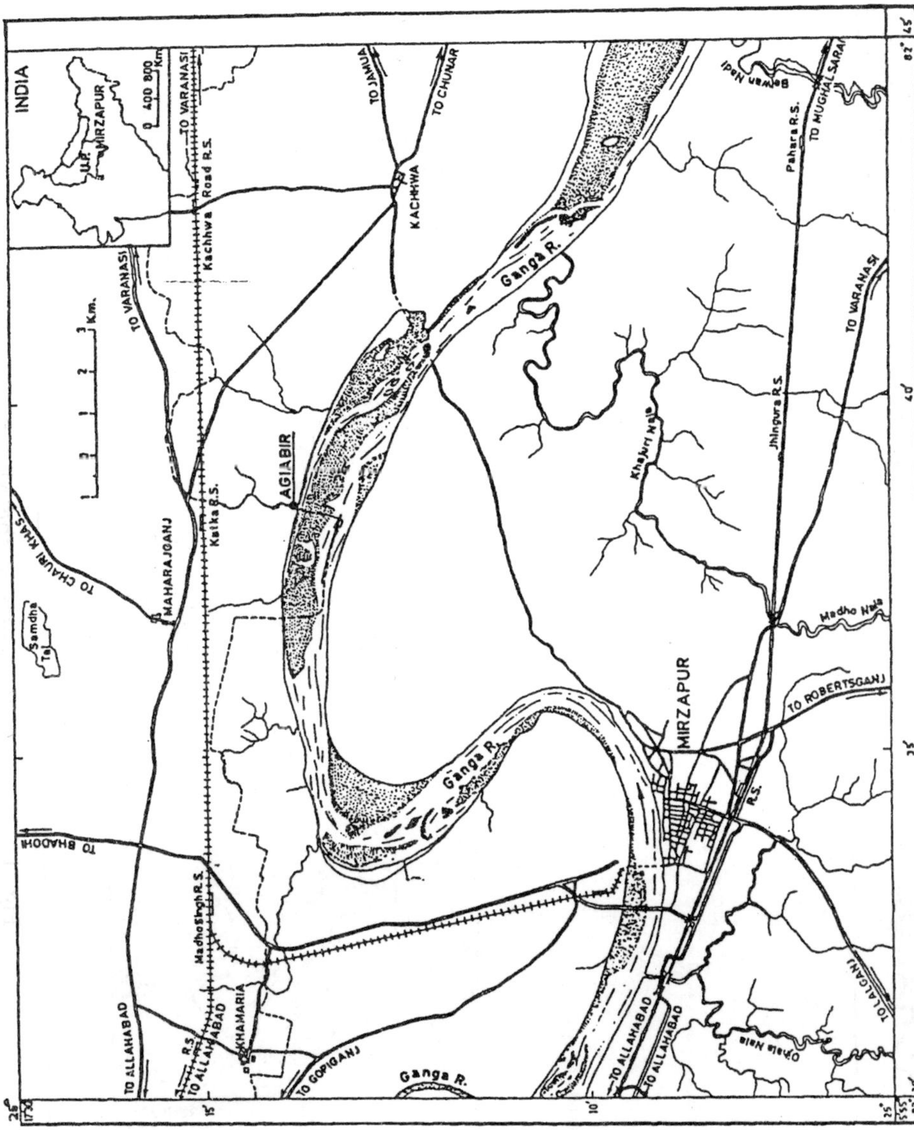

Fig. 2. Location map of Agiabir.

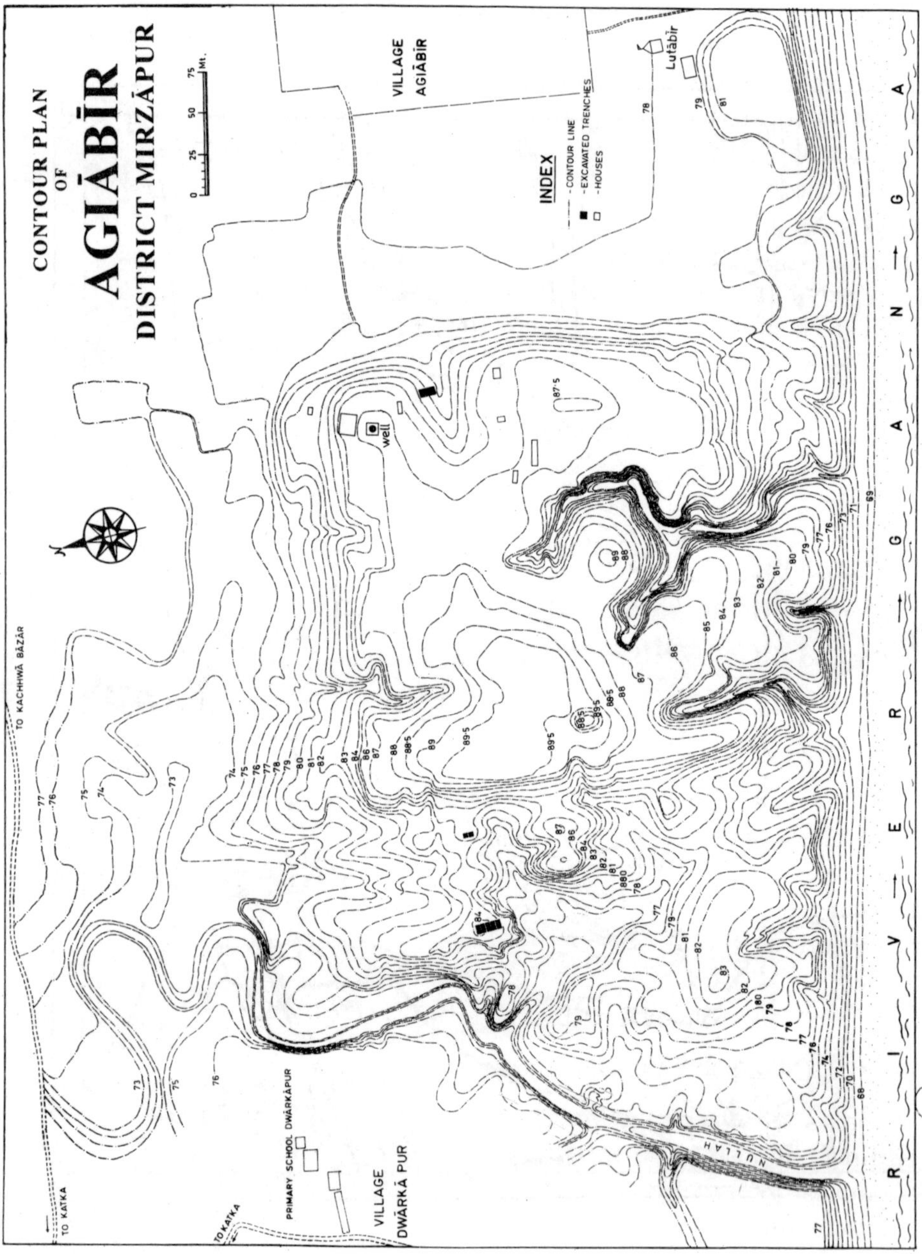

Fig. 3. Contour plan of Agiabir.

LOCATION AND DISCOVERY OF THE SITE

The protohistoric settlement of Agiabir (Latitude 25° 13′ 52^{2} N; Longitude 82° 38′ 41^{2} E) was discovered in 1998-99 (Singh, 1998-99) and it was subjected to archaeological excavations for three field seasons (1999-2001) by the Banaras Hindu University under the direction of the authors. This settlement is located on the left bank of the Ganga, near Katka railway station on the Varanasi-Allahabad section of the Northern Railway in district Mirzapur of eastern Uttar Pradesh (Fig. 2). The ancient settlement extends in an area of more than a kilometre along the river and it has been partly eroded by it (Fig. 3). The main mound alone measures about 500 m x 500 m (Pl. I-A). Excavation was carried out by the present team in the western part of the settlement (named ABR-1) as also in the eastern part of the main mound (termed ABR-2) during 1998-99. On Mound-1 ten trenches, measuring 3 m x 3 m square were excavated (Pl. I-B) and an interim report has already been published (Singh & Singh, 1999; Singh & Singh, 2000 : 31-68). These excavations resulted into the documentation of the following culture-sequence :

Period I	:	Narhan culture (1300 BC - 900 BC)
Period II	:	Pre NBPW with Iron (900 BC - 600 BC)
Period III	:	NBPW culture (600 BC - 200 BC)
Period IV	:	Sunga-Kushana Period (200 BC - AD 300)
Period V	:	Gupta and post Gupta deposits (AD 300 - AD 700)

In the second and third season excavation was conducted in a 20 m x 20 m area on the southern part of the main mound which resulted in the discovery of a large house-complex of burnt bricks, datable to Period IV. It comprized 11 rooms of various sizes having altogether 5 building levels (Singh & Singh, 2001 : 157-159)

STRATA, PERIODS AND POTTERY

(I) PERIOD I (NARHAN CULTURE)

The remains of Narhan culture were documented in the lowermost 60 cm cultural deposit. The inhabitants of this period lived in wattle-and-daub houses. Fragments of burnt clay with reed marks and patches of floors, ovens and post-holes have been recorded. Two silos, obviously used for storage of grains, were recorded from this period (Pl. II-A).

The main ceramic industries of this period comprized Black-and-Red Ware (mostly medium and coarse fabrics), black slipped ware (in a limited quantity but in fine fabric) and red ware. A few sherds of Black-and-Red

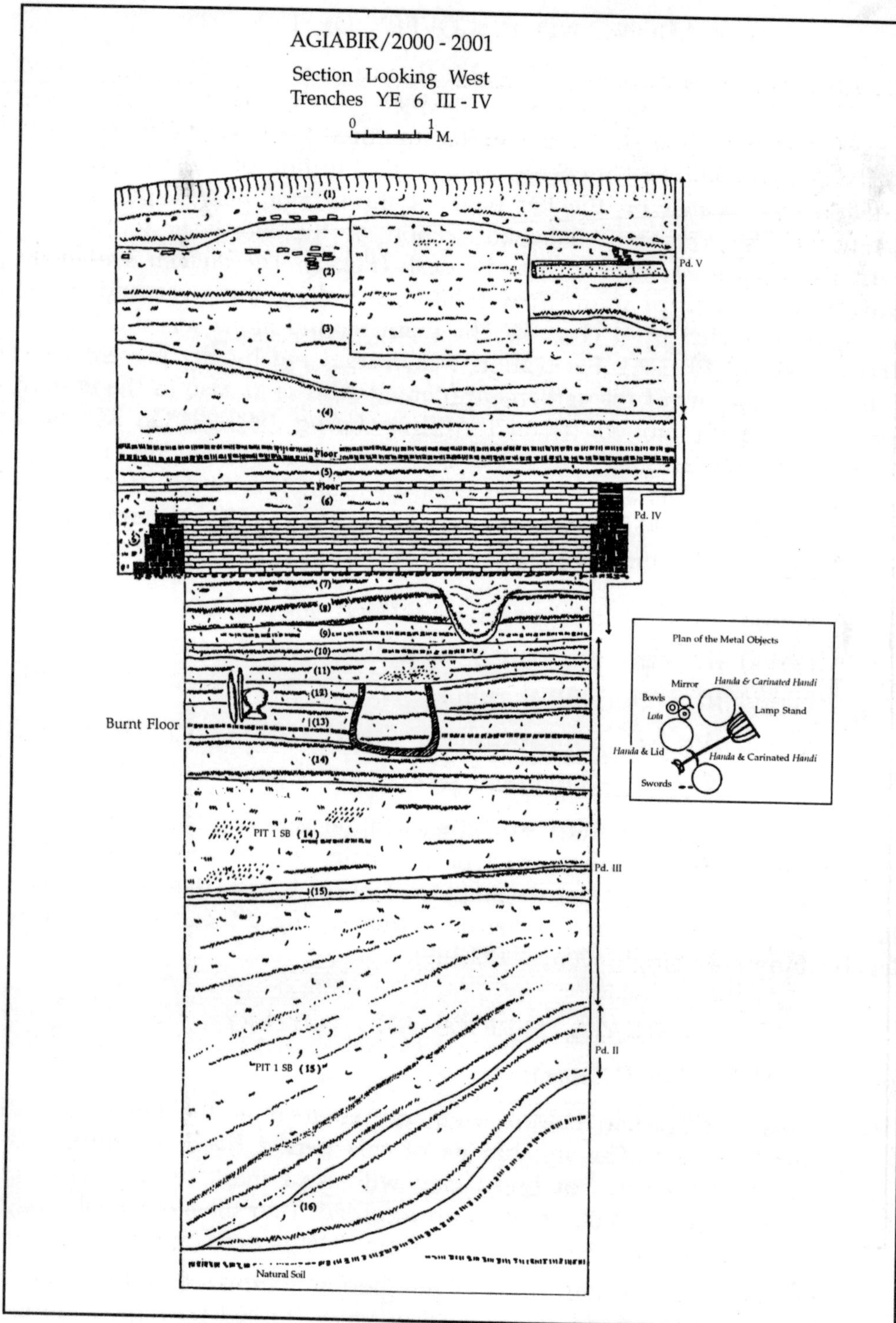

Fig. 4. Section of trenches YE6 III & IV.

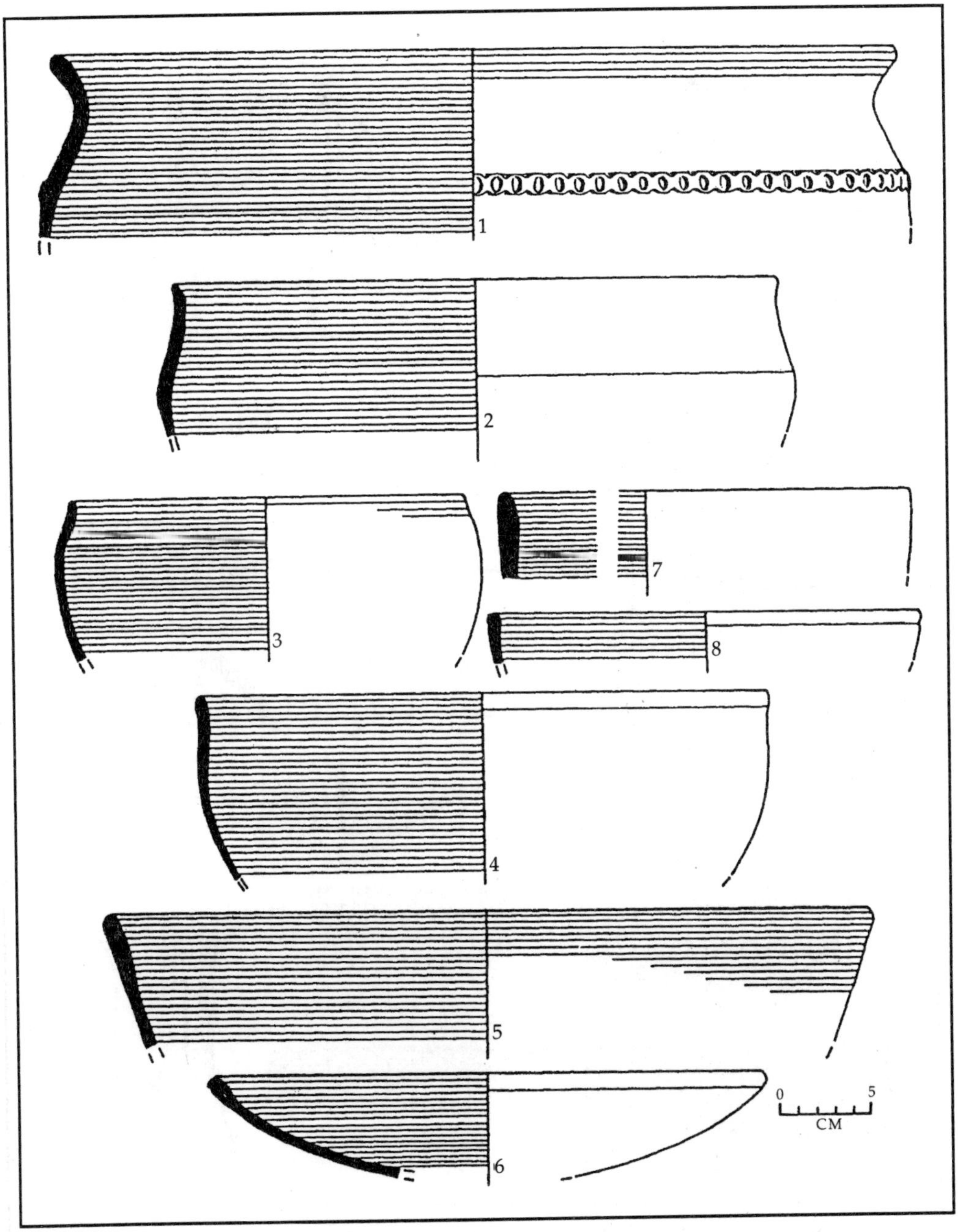

Fig. 5. Bowls and basins of Black-and-Red Ware, Period I.

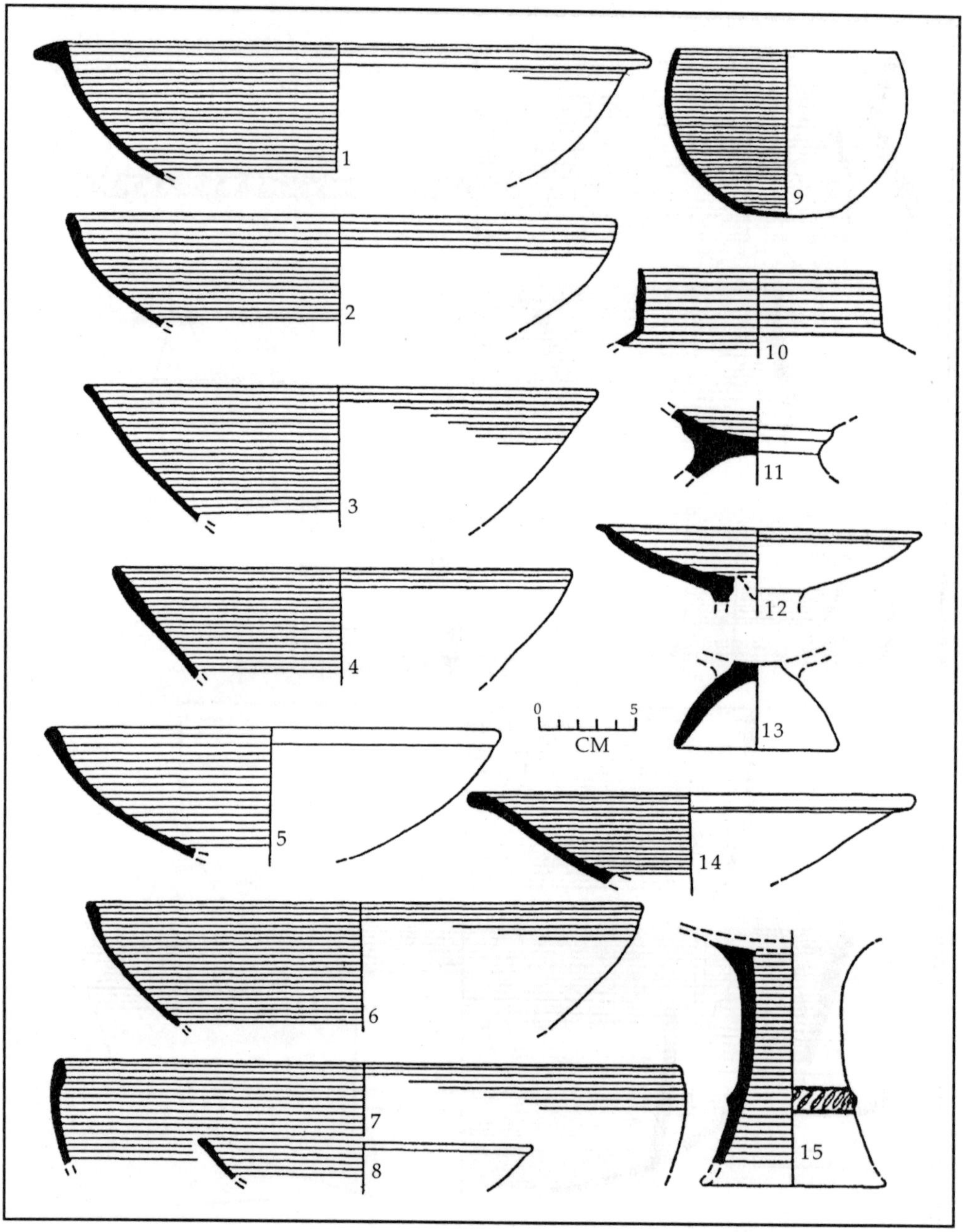

Fig. 6. Bowls and basins of Black-and-Red Ware, Period I.

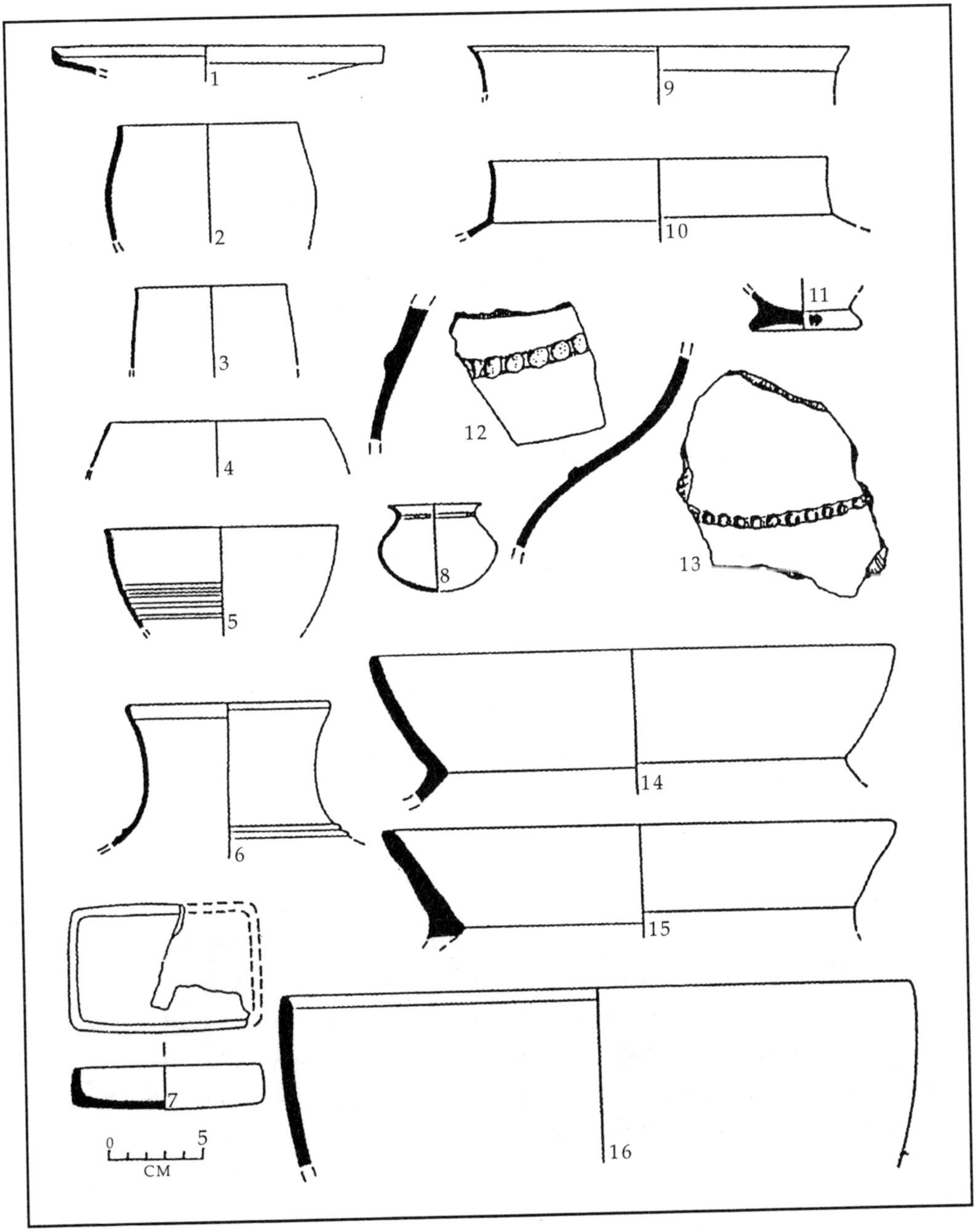

Fig. 7. Black Slipped Ware and Red Ware, Period I.

1-11 : Various types of vessels of Black Slipped Ware, Period I; 12-16 : Vases and basins of Red Ware, Period I

Ware and black slipped ware bear linear paintings in white as in the case of Narhan. The main types of Black-and-Red Ware are bowls, storage jars, lipped basins and dish-on-stand (Figs. 5-6). Some sherds of Black-and-Red Ware bear cord impressions on the exterior. In black slipped ware the important shapes are deep bowls, *lota* shaped vessels and pedestal bowls (Fig. 7). In red ware no kitchen ware vessels are reported except for legged perforated bowls with several perforations at the base (Fig. 8, Nos. 1-3). Vases and storage jars, some bearing applique designs on the exterior, are the other types in this ware. Some of the important shapes of the above-noted ceramic industries are illustrated below:

FIG. 5

1. Basin of Black-and-Red Ware with applique design on the exterior at the point of carination. A chain pattern has been executed on the added strip of the clay. This vessel has bright slip on both sides, medium fabric. From Period I.
2. Basin of Black-and-Red Ware with everted rim and globular body, medium fabric. From Period I.
3. Fragment of a bowl of Black-and-Red Ware with round rim and convex sides, medium fabric. From Period I.
4. Bowl of Black-and-Red Ware with flaring rim, convex sides, thick slip on the interior, medium fabric. From Period I.
5. Deep basin of Black-and-Red Ware with externally thickened rim, straight sides. The black colour of the interior extends below the rim, coarse fabric. From Period I.
6. Shallow platter of Black-and-Red Ware with internally thickened rim, weak carination at the neck and bright slip, both on the exterior and interior of the vessel. Similar shape in Black-and-Red Ware occurs in Period I at Narhan (Singh, 1994, Fig. 21, No. 81).
7. Fragment of deep bowl of Black-and-Red Ware with externally thickened rim, straight sides, medium fabric. From Period I.
8. Bowl of Black-and-Red Ware with internally bevelled rim, tapering profile, medium fabric. From Period I.

FIG. 6

1. Hemispherical basin with flared externally thickened rim, flattened from the top, sharp carination at the neck, coarse fabric. From Period I. Similar vessels occur in Period I at Narhan (Singh, 1994, Fig. 23, No. 1).

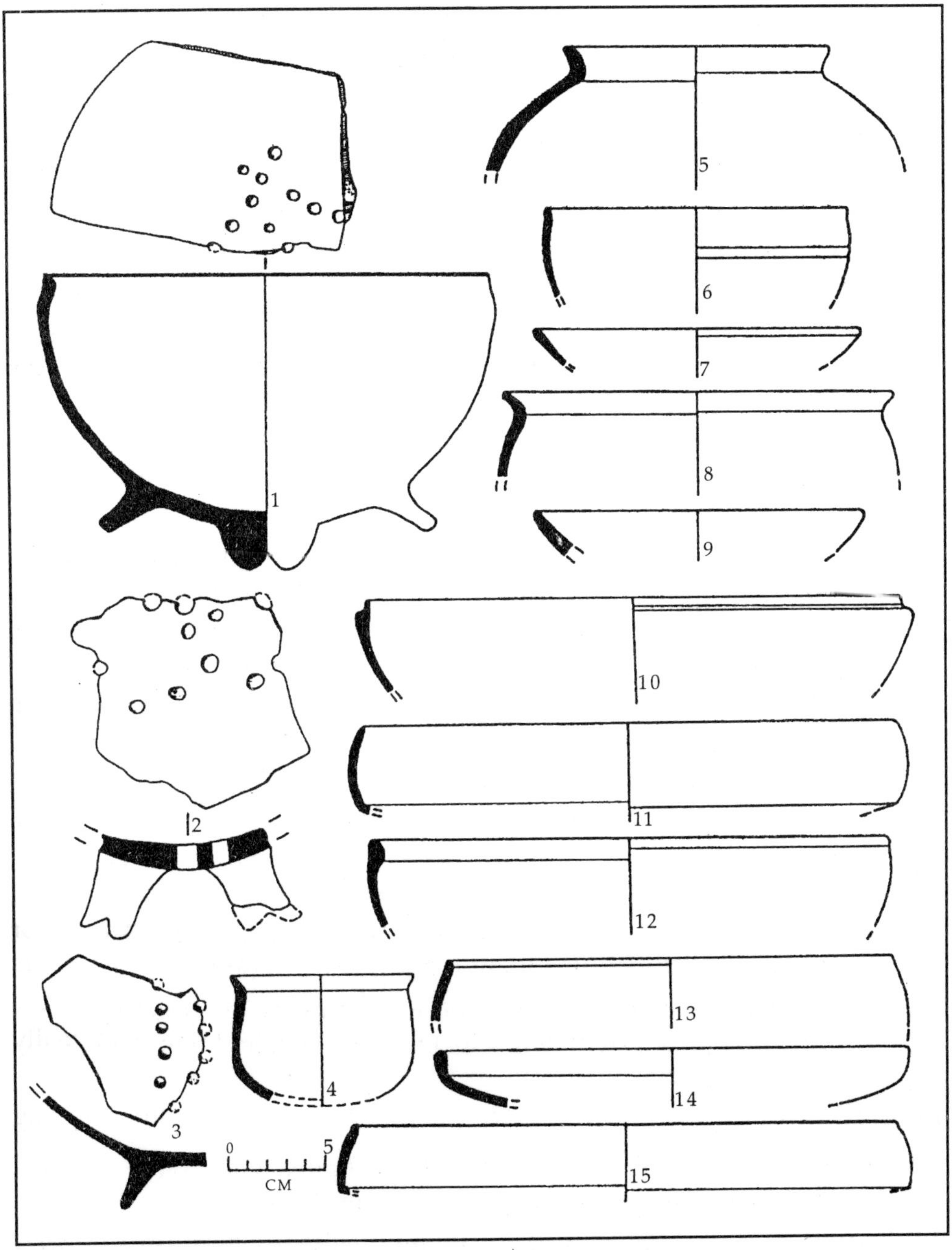

Fig. 8. Red Ware, Periods I & II.

1-3 : Perforated Bowls of Red Ware, Period I; 4-9 : Bowls of Red Ware, Period II; 10-11 & 14-15 : Bowl and dish of Red Ware, Period II; 12-13 : Bowls of Red Ware, Period II

2. Fragment of a shallow bowl of Black-and-Red Ware with internally thickened rim, convex sides, medium fabric. From Period I.
3. Bowl of Black-and-Red Ware with internally sharpened rim, tapering sides, medium fabric. From Period I.
4. Fragment of a bowl of Black-and-Red Ware with externally thickened rim and convex sides. It has a bright slip on both sides. From Period I.
5. Same as No. 2 above.
6. Bowl of Black-and-Red Ware with collared rim, tapering sides, medium fabric. From Period I.
7. Bowl of Black-and-Red Ware with round rim and convex sides. It has back slip on the exterior upto the neck, medium fabric. From Period I.
8. Fragment of a shallow platter of Black-and-Red Ware with externally thickened rim, convex sides, medium fabric. From Period I.
9. Bowl with featureless rim and rounded sides. From period I.
10. Vase of Black-and-Red Ware with vertical internally sharpened rim and globular profile, medium fabric. From Period I. Similar shapes occur in Black-and-Red Ware & black slipped ware in Period I at Narhan (Singh, 1994, fig. 21, No. 71 and fig. 27 Nos. 21-22).
11. Middle portion of a pedestalled bowl of Black-and-Red Ware, medium fabric. From Period I.
12. Upper portion of a pedestalled bowl of Black-and-Red Ware with flaring rim, medium fabric. From Period I.
13. Lower portion of a pedestalled bowl of Black-and-Red Ware. From Period I.
14. Upper portion of a pedestalled bowl of Black-and-Red Ware with flaring thickened rim, medium fabric. From Period I.
15. Fragment of a stem of Black-and-Red Ware with grooves on the exterior. It has a bright red slip on the exterior. From Period I.

FIG. 7

1. Fragment of a shallow platter of black slipped ware with vertically cut rim, tapering sides, fine fabric. From Period I.
2. Bowl of black slipped ware with internally bevelled rim, tapering sides, fine fabric. From Period I.
3. Bowl of black slipped ware with featureless rim, straight sides, fine fabric. From Period I.

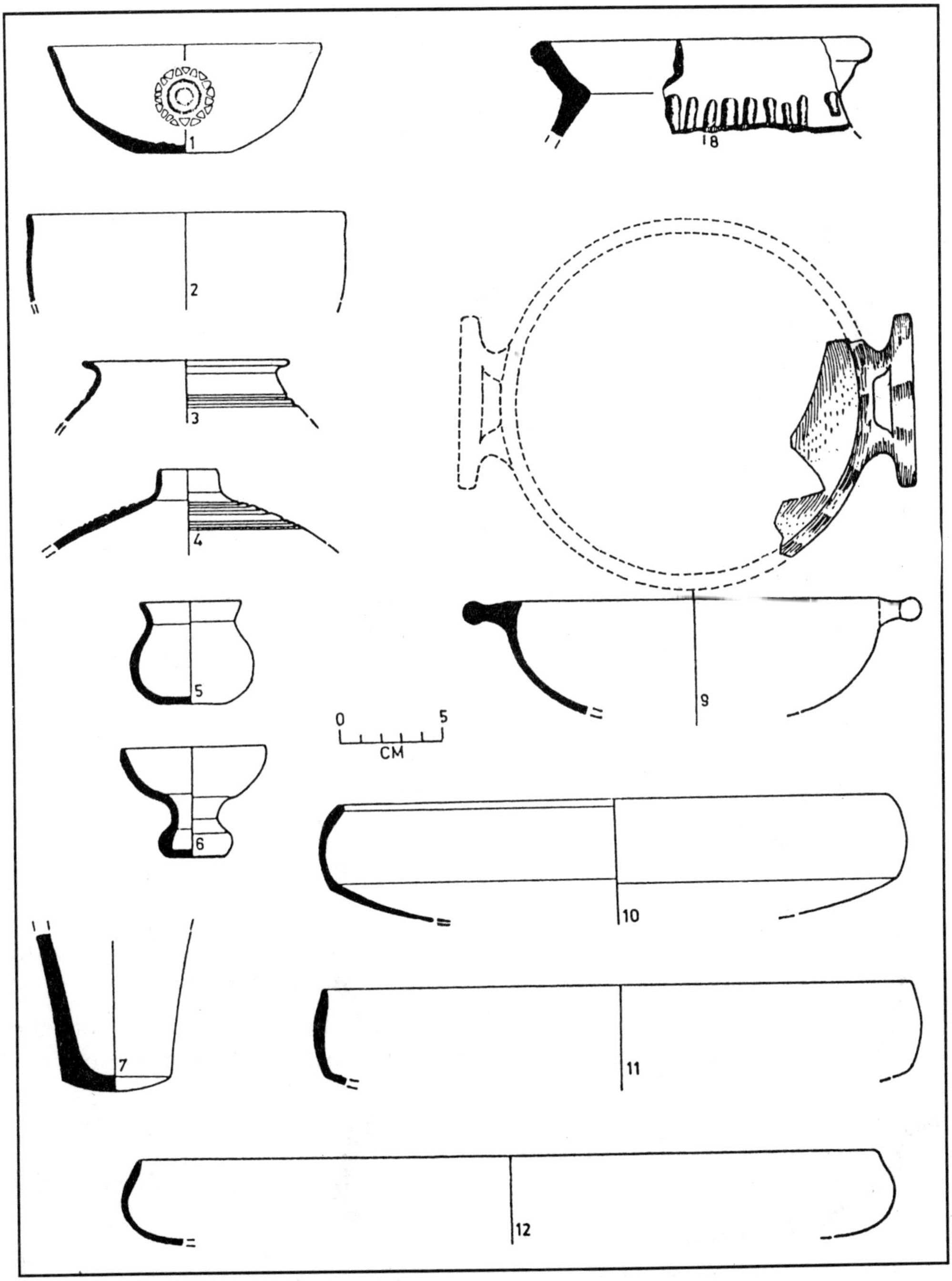

Fig. 9. Grey Ware, Black Slipped Ware, NBP Ware and Red Ware, Period III.
1 : Bowls of Grey Ware, Period III; 2 : Bowl of Black Slipped Ware, Period III; 3-8 : Vase and tumbler of Red Ware, Period III; 9-12 : Dishes of NBP Ware, Period III

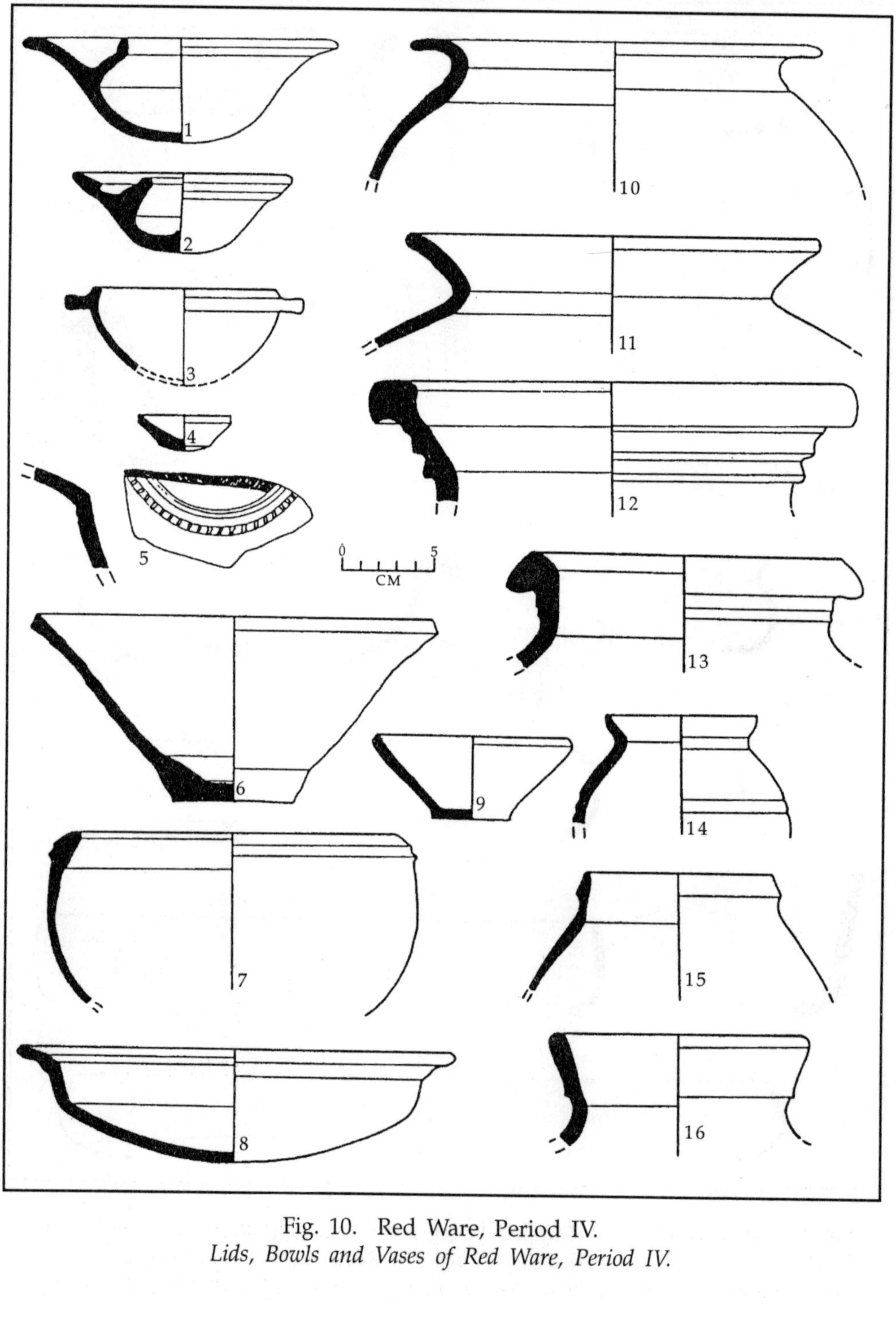

Fig. 10. Red Ware, Period IV.
Lids, Bowls and Vases of Red Ware, Period IV.

Pl. IA. General view of the mounds.

Pl. IB. Excavated trenches on mound 1.

Pl. IIA. Silo for storage of grains, Period I.

Pl. IIB. Bead manufacturing workshop, Period I.

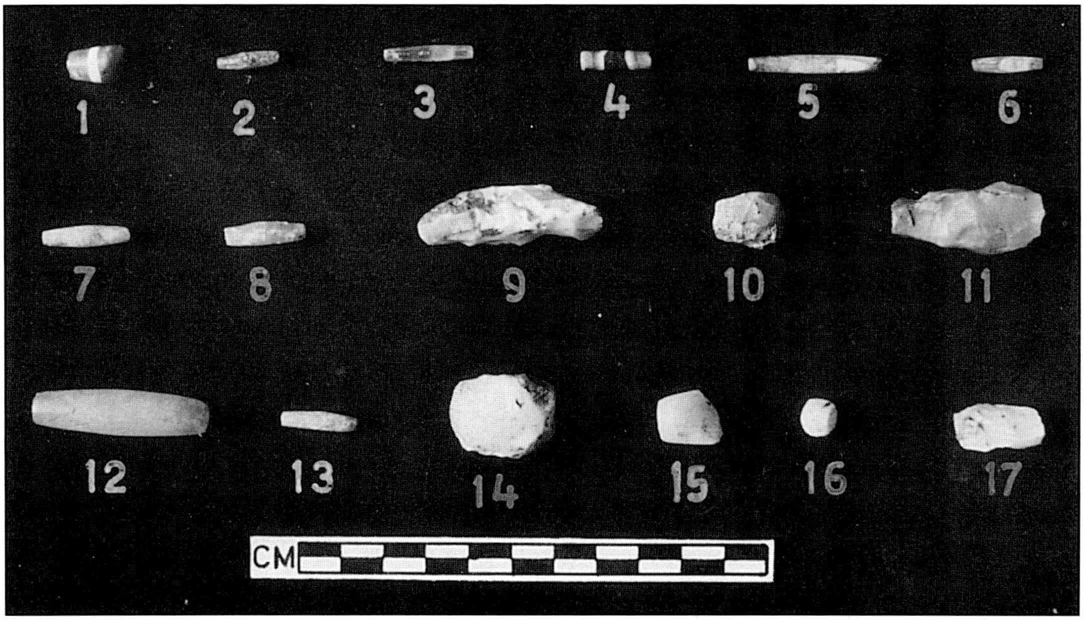

Pl. IIIA. Unfinished stone beads, Period I.

Pl. IIIB. Unfinished stone beads of Periods II & III.

Pl. IVA. Rammed floor with post-holes, Period II.

Pl. IVB. Rammed floor of Period III.

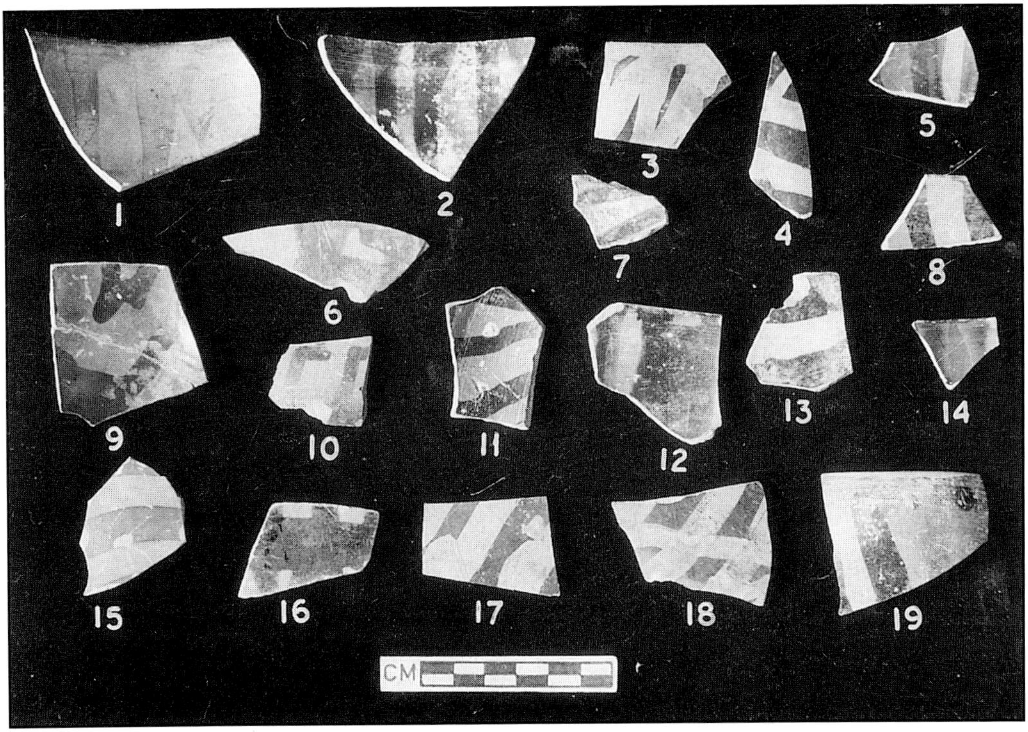

Pl. VA. Painted NBP Ware, Period III.

Pl. VB. Dish of NBP Ware, Period III.

Pl. VIA. Vases of Red Ware with applique designs, Period III.

Pl. VIB. General view of structures, Period IV.

Pl. VIIA. View of a room with floor, Period IV.

Pl. VIIB. A view of Room No. 1, Period IV.

Pl. VIIIA. A view of the same from the east, Period IV.

Pl. VIIIB. A room of burnt bricks of Period IV.

4. Same as above but bigger in size.
5. Fragment of a bowl of black slipped ware with externally sharpened rim with internal ridges, fine fabric. From Period I.
6. High necked vase of black slipped ware with splayed out featureless rim, medium fabric. From Period I.
7. Lamp / Incense burner (?) of ill baked clay. From Period I. Similar specimen occurs in the Chalcolithic level at Inamgaon (Dhavalikar *et al.*, 1988, Fig. 13.50, Nos. 1-3).
8. Miniature vessel of black slipped ware with three perforations. From Period I.
9. Deep bowl of black slipped ware with everted sharpened rim with a groove on the exterior, fine fabric. From Period I.
10. *Lota* of black slipped ware with vertical sharpened rim and bulging body. It bears a bright slip on the exterior, medium fabric. From Period I.
11. Fragment of a pedestalled bowl of black slipped ware with flat base. From Period I.
12. Fragment of a vase of red ware with applique design on the exterior.
13. Same as above.
14. Vase of red ware with internally thickened rim, sharp carination at the neck. It bears a bright red slip on the exterior. From Period I.
15. Same as above but with flaring rim. From Period I.
16. Fragment of a deep basin of red slipped ware with featureless rim, straight sides, medium fabric. From Period I.

A bead manufacturing workshop is an important discovery of this period (Pl. II-B). Twenty-four stone beads (16 finished and 08 unfinished), one bead each of bone and shell together with waste stone chips were recovered (Pl. III-A). Among the beads made of semi-precious stones, agate was the most favoured material and the presence of unfinished beads of this stone right in the earliest period demonstrates that they were manufactured locally (Pl. III). This tradition of bead making was continued in the subsequent two periods as well (Pl. III-B). It would thus be logical to conclude that bead manufacturing was an important industry and obviously they were exported to other contemporary settlements, besides catering to the aesthetic requirements of the local inhabitants. Faience was another interesting material and its presence in sizeable numbers, particularly in Period III is an important discovery, indicating its local manufacture and trade (Singh & Singh, 2000 : 141-149). The inhabitants of Period I at Agiabir made the best use of the neighbouring Vindhyan hills. The easy accessibility of siliceous stones in the hills opposite this site led to the manufacture of beads and microliths locally.

Among the other noteworthy finds of this period are the microliths including blades, cores, bladelets, retouchers and flakes. This industry comprises chips, flakes, bladelets, cores and retouchers (Fig. 22). Besides, some stone nodules were also found. The stone lumps used here are banded agate, chert, jasper, quartz and chalcedony(Singh, 2000 : 57-63).

Other antiquities comprise seventeen terracotta beads (Pl. XXIV), 34 gamesmen (Pl. XXIX-B), nine bone points (Pl. XXVII-A) and 63 pottery discs (with ten perforated specimens) (Pl. XXIX-A).

An incense burner or lamp of baked clay is a noteworthy find of this period (Fig. 7, No. 7). Only one fish-hook of copper was recovered (Pl. XIII-B-1). No iron objects was found.

The inhabitants of Agiabir were not entirely vegetarians. Food was supplemented by meat as indicated by the discovery of a large numbers of animal bones with cut marks. Fire places along with charred bones provide adequate evidence for the roasting of meat. Four charcoal samples were collected from various strata of Period I. Their study will provide valuable evidence about the fauna and chronology of this period.

PERIOD II (PRE-NBPW WITH IRON)

As in the preceding period, the inhabitants of this period also continued to live in wattle-and-daub houses. Traces of burnt floors, ovens, silos and post-holes have been recorded (Pl. IV). This period is marked by the ceramic assemblage of black slipped ware and red ware but total absence of Black-and-Red Ware. The main types in the black slipped ware are knife edged bowls, dishes and pedestal bowls. In red ware dishes, knife edged bowls, tumbler with thick core, button based goblets and vases are the principal types (Fig. 8, Nos. 4-15). The small finds comprise beads of semi-precious stones as well as terracotta (Pls. XXII-B & XXIV-B), gamesman, bone points, antlers, iron and copper objects and pottery discs. The principal shapes of the red ware of this period are illustrated below :

FIG. 8

1. Fragment of a perforated bowl of red ware with four legs and eleven perforations at the bottom. From Period I. Similar vessels occur at Narhan, Imlidih Khurd, Khairadih, Hastinapura and Atranjikhera.
2. *Ibid*.

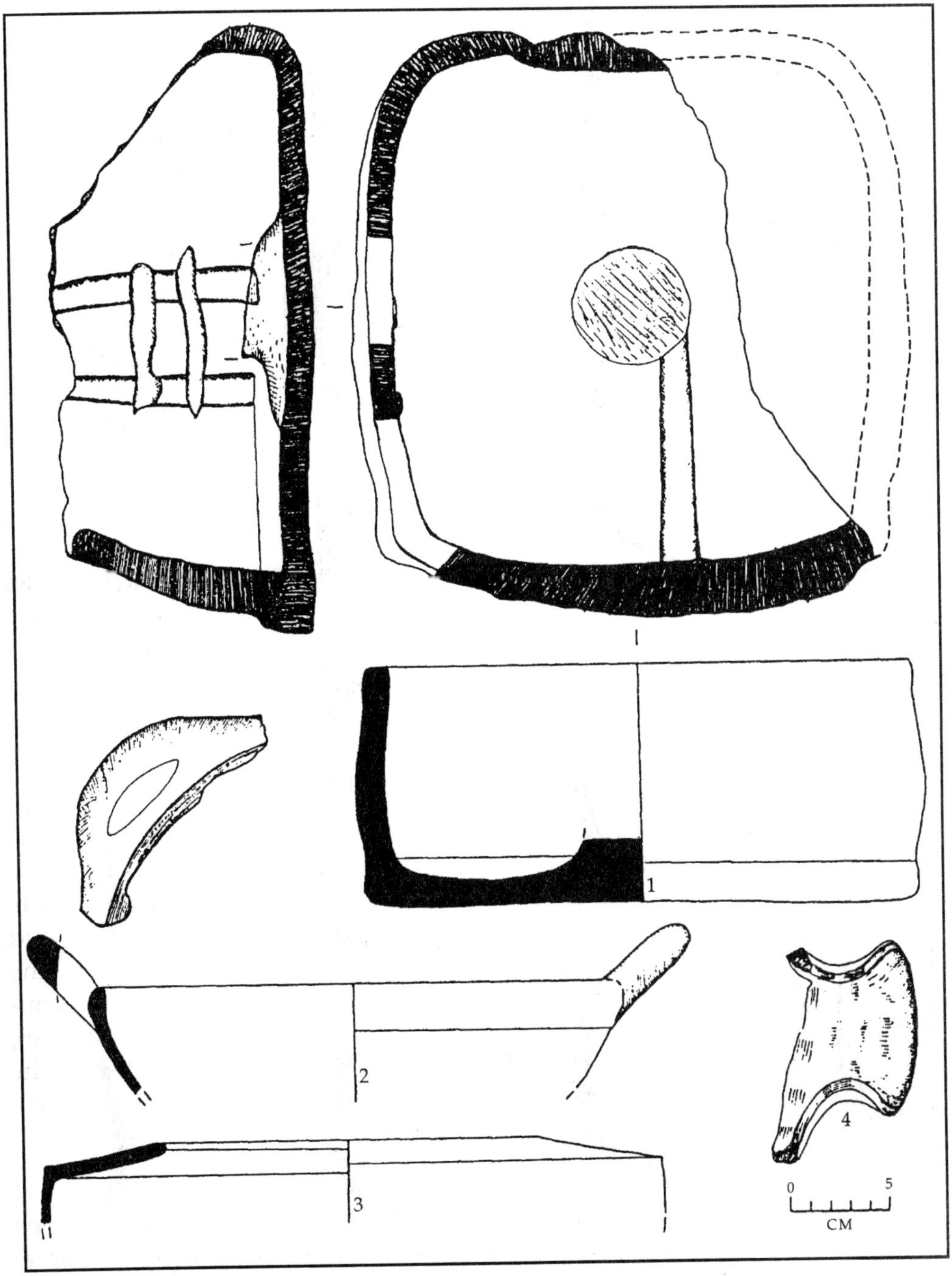

Fig. 11. Votive tank, *Karāhī*, carinated *hāndī* and lipped basin of Red Ware, Period IV.

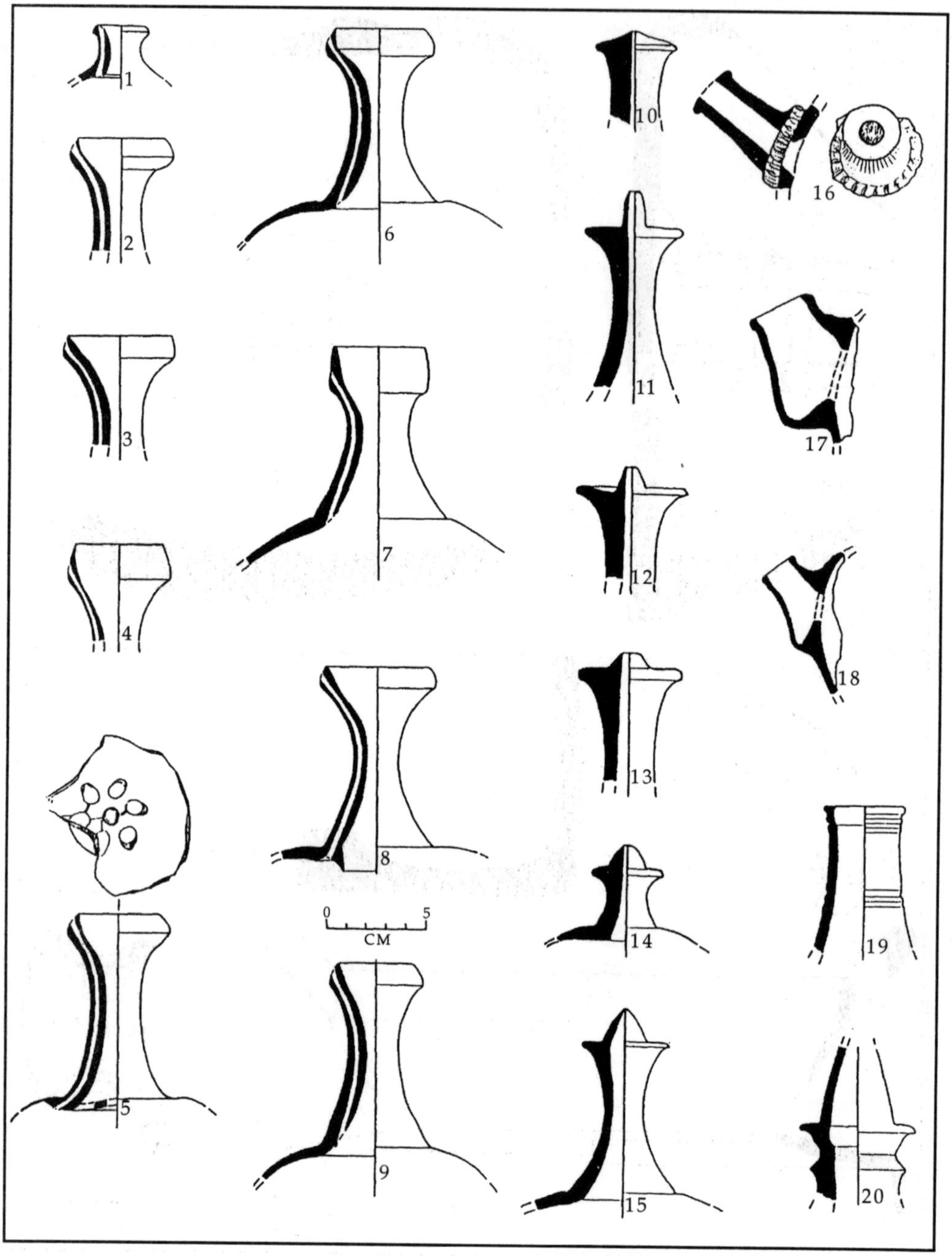

Fig. 12. Red Ware, bottle-necked jars and sprinklers, Period IV.

3. *Ibid.*
4. Bowl of red ware with everted, rounded rim and straight sides. From Period II.
5. Vase of red ware with short flaring rim and globular body, medium fabric. From Period II.
6. Bowl of red ware with internally sharpened rim and convex sides. From Period II.
7. Shallow bowl of red ware with internally sharpened rim and convex sides. From Period II.
8. Fragment of a bowl of red ware with everted, rounded rim, straight sides. From Period II.
9. Same as No. 7.
10. Flanged bowl of black slipped ware with sharpened rim and convex sides. From Period II.
11. Dish of black slipped ware with incurved rounded rim and convex sides. From Period II.
12. Fragment of a bowl of red ware with collared rim, convex sides, medium fabric. From Period II.
13. Fragment of a bowl of red ware with internally sharpened rim and rounded sides, medium fabric. From Period II.
14. Shallow dish of black slipped ware with internally thickened rim, medium fabric. From Period II.
15. Fragment of a dish of black slipped ware with closing rim, medium fabric. From Period II.

PERIOD III (NBPW PERIOD)

As in the preceding period, the inhabitants of this period also lived in wattle-and-daub houses. Remains of post-holes, ovens, rammed floors made of pot sherds were noticed (Pl. IV-B). The main ceramic industries of this period are black slipped ware, NBPW, some of it of deluxe variety having silvery, golden, pink and steel blue shades, grey ware and red ware. A good quantity of painted sherds of NBPW were recovered (Pl. V-A). Straight sided and flanged bowls, dishes with incurved rim are the important types in the first three wares (Fig. 9). In the red ware bowls, lipped basins and vases (with appliqué design) are the main types (Pl. VI-A). A dish of NBPW with handle and bearing a thick slip is an important discovery of this period (Pl. V-B, Fig. 9, No. 9). This type has not been reported from any other site so far. Important shapes of grey ware, black slipped ware, NBPW and red ware are illustrated below :

FIG. 9

1. Bowl of grey ware with externally thickened flaring rim and slightly tapering sides, decorated with stamp design, medium fabric. From Period III.
2. Fragment of a bowl of black slipped ware with vertical internally sharpened rim and convex sides, medium fabric. From Period III.
3. Vase of red ware with vertical externally collared rim, carinated neck, globular profile, medium fabric. From Period III.
4. Vase of red ware with short and narrow mouth and featureless rim, globular body, several grooves on the exterior below the rim, medium fabric. From Period III.
5. Miniature vase of red ware with splayed out rim, globular body, medium fabric. From Period III.
6. A complete specimen of footed bowl of red ware with featureless rim, medium fabric. From Period III.
7. Fragment of tumbler of red ware, medium fabric. From Period III.
8. Vase of red ware with splayed out externally thickened rim, medium fabric. From Period III.
9. Dish of NBPW with elongated handle, fine fabric, From Period III. It is a new shape, not reported from any other site (Plate-VI).
10. Fragment of dish of black slipped ware with internally thickened rim, medium fabric. From Period III.
11. Dish of black slipped ware with internally bevelled rim and sides carinated to a sagger base. From Period III.
12. Same as No. 10.

The discovery of a number of unfinished beads along with stone chips from this period indicates that these were produced locally (Pl. III-B).

The small finds comprise beads of terracotta and semi-precious stones (agate, carnelian, quartz and faience) (Pl. XXIII-A); bone points, terracotta balls, copper and iron objects and terracotta discs. Mention may be made of the discovery of unusually large number of terracotta discs (182 in number) found in the limited excavations (Pl. XXX-B). Among these, three terracotta discs bear running antelope motif incised on them (Pl. XXX-B, Nos. 3, 10, 15). Similar specimens were recorded earlier from Rajghat (Narain & Singh, 1977, Plate IX, No. 8) and Prahladpur (Narain & Roy, 1968, Fig. 20, No. 18).

PERIOD IV (SUNGA-KUSHANA PERIOD)

Period IV belongs to the Sunga-Kushana period. The houses of this period were made of burnt bricks. The structural activity shows three phases. In the upper phase structures were largely built of reused material and followed more or less the earlier plan (Pl. VII-A). As stated earlier, a house complex of 11 rooms with a courtyard and a boundary wall was noticed (Pl. VI-B). The plinth area of this complex is 18 m 50 cm (east-west) and 12 m 80 cm (north-south). There were two entrances to this structure, one from the south-east corner and other from northern side. The internal measurement of each of room is given below:

Room No. 1	:	6.20 m x 2.40 m
Room No. 2	:	3.70 m x 2.40 m
Room No. 3	:	2.90 m x 2.50 m
Room No. 4	:	5.15 m x 2.50 m
Room No. 5	:	2.30 m x 2.20 m
Room No. 6	:	2.60 m x 2.30 m
Room No. 7	:	2.00 m x 1.50 m
Room No. 8	:	3.05 m x 2.24 m
Room No. 9	:	2.90 m x 2.24 m
Room No. 10	:	3.40 m x 2.30 m
Room No. 11	:	2.50 m x 2.00 m

Room Nos. 1 and 4 are rectangular in size and measure 6.20 x 2.40 and 5.15 x 2.50 metre respectively. The bricks used in these rooms and in the boundary wall are of 44 x 29 x 5 cm, 39 x 28 x 5 cm and 42 x 28 x 5 cm size. Three ovens made of burnt bricks were noticed in Room Nos. 2, 8 and 9. Floors made of burnt bricks were exposed in Room No. 1 and in the courtyard (Pls. VII-A, VII-B). This courtyard was used in two phases. In the first constructional phase the house contained as many as 11 rooms, all around a central courtyard which is rammed. In the subsequent phase the area of the courtyard was increased by demolishing Room Nos. 3, 4 and annexing this area into the courtyard. The courtyard which had a rammed base earlier, was now provided with a pavement of burnt bricks.

One room measuring 2.98 x 2.20 m with walls made of burnt bricks (size 46 x 26 x 5 cm) was exposed in the trench located on the eastern slope of the main mound (Pl. VIII-B). The northern and western parts of this structure were found to be robbed.

A fragmentary nude female figurine with legs raised and spread apart, recovered from the room is a noteworthy find (Pl. IX-A). Similar figures were reported earlier from Bhita (Marshall, 1915, 24-94), Kausambi and Jhusi. This indicates that the cult of mother goddess was prevalent in the Middle Ganga Plain in the early centuries of the Christian era.

Small finds of this period comprized terracotta human and animal figurines (Pls. XXXI, XXXII, XXXIII), beads of semi-precious stones and terracotta, terracotta discs, antimony rods of copper, iron objects and bone points. A votive tank of terracotta is a noteworthy find of this period (Pl. IX). Three ringwells of this period were exposed (Pls. X-A, B).

Thirty-six copper coins were recovered from these rooms in different layers, of which 16 coins were recovered from Room No. 4 alone (Pls. XI-A, B). A number of terracotta lids were recovered from this period (Pl. XII-A).

The ceramic industry comprized red ware with vase, ink pot lid, pear-shaped vase (Ahichhatra 10 A) and lugged *karāhī* as the main types. In the red polished ware bottle-necked jars with small perforation in the body to control the flow of liquid (sprinklers) as the main type (Pl. XII-B, Fig. 12). The limited excavation yielded 28 pieces of neck portion of the sprinklers. Similar pieces, seemingly in limited number, were found at Kausambi (Sharma, 1969 : fig. 31 types 118-119) and Sringaverapura (Lal, 1993 : fig. 29). The important shapes are illustrated below :

FIG. 10

1. Lid of red ware with closing featureless rim. Of medium fabric. From Period IV.
2. Same as above but smaller in size. From Period IV.
3. Lid with a flat waist, medium fabric. From Period IV.
4. A miniature bowl of red ware. From Period IV.
5. Fragment of a vase of red ware. decorated in panel, medium fabric. From Period IV.
6. A complete specimen of bowl of red ware, slightly everted bevelled rim and sides progressively thickened towards a thick flat base. From Period IV.
7. Basin with externally collared rim and a groove on the neck. From Period IV.
8. Dish / lid of red ware with tapering sides and a sagger base. From Period IV.

Pl. IXA. A nude terracotta female figurine (mother goddess) from Period IV.

Pl. IXB. A votive tank, Period IV.

Pl. XA. Ringwell of Period IV.

Pl. XB. Ringwell of Period IV.

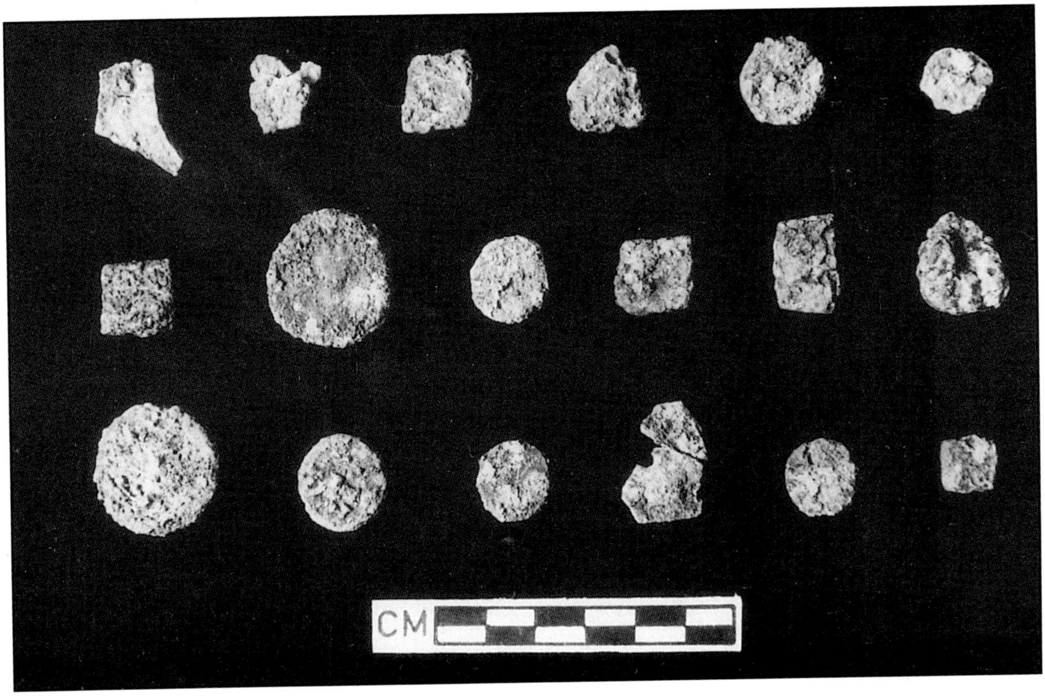

Pl. XIA. Copper coins of Period IV.

Pl. XIB. Copper coins of Period IV.

Pl. XIIA. Terracotta lids of Period IV.

Pl. XIIB. Bottle-necked jars of Period IV.

Pl. XIIIA. Hearth from Period V.

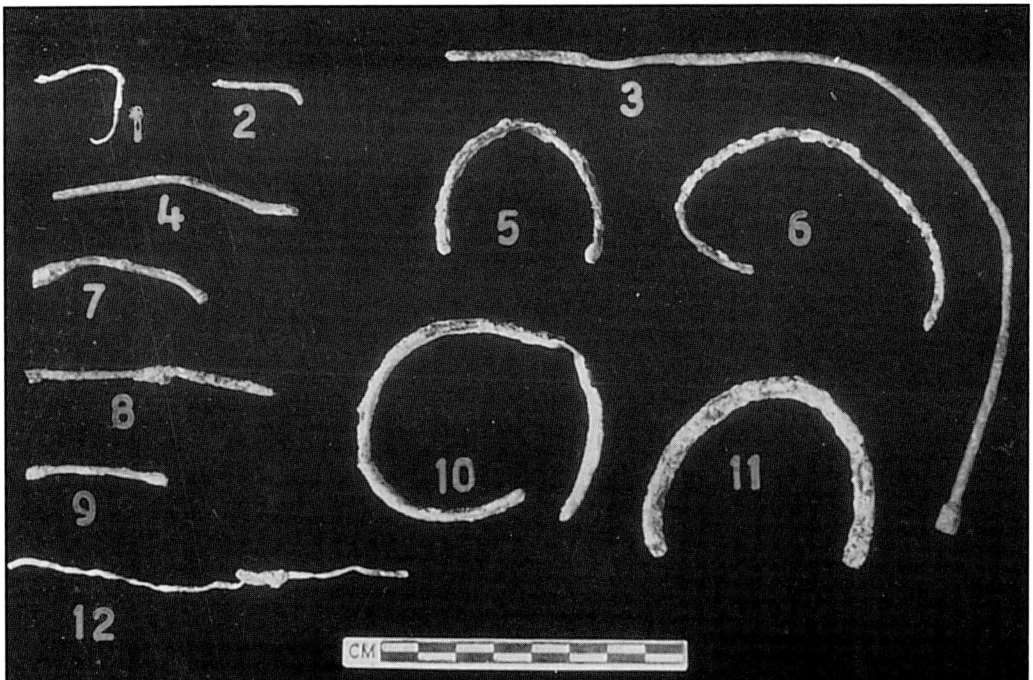

Pl. XIIIB. Copper objects of Periods I & III.

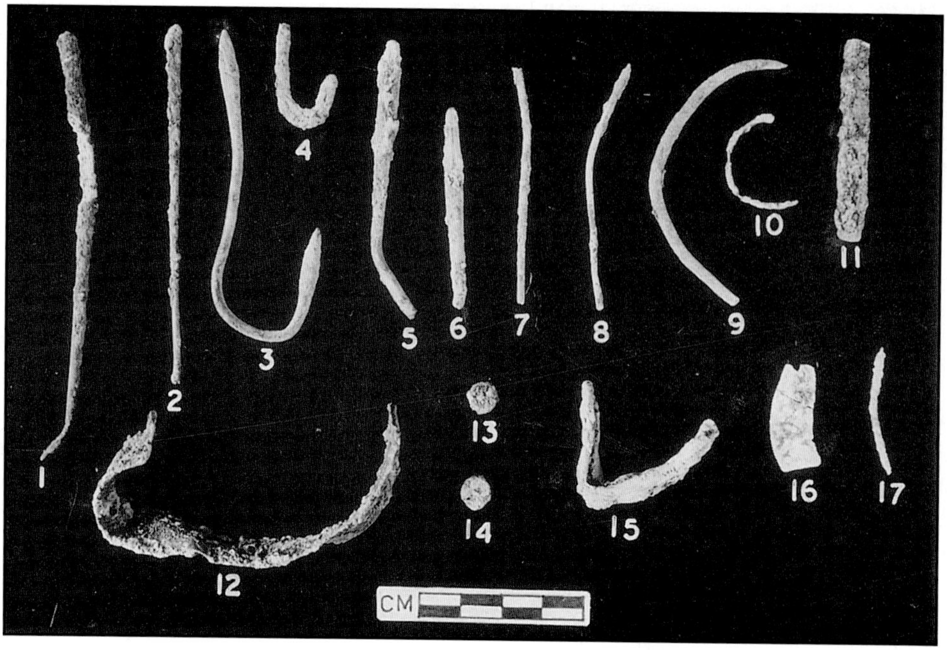

Pl. XIVA. Copper objects of Period III.

Pl. XIVB. Copper and iron objects *in situ*, Period III.

Pl. XVA. Copper bowl of Period III.

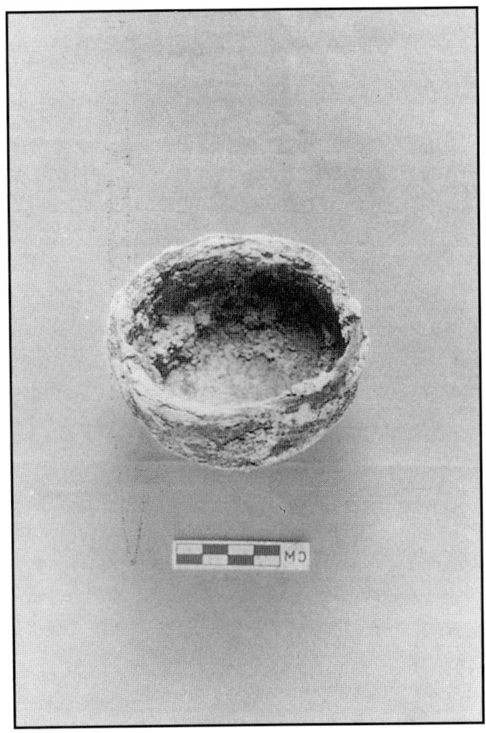

Pl. XVB. Miniature copper bowl of Period III.

Pl. XVIA. Cooking vessel (*Hāndā*) of copper, Period III.

Pl. XVIB. Cooking vessel (*Hāndā*) of copper, Period III.

9. Bowl of dull red ware with internally thickened rim. From Period IV.
10. Vase of red slipped ware with collared rim, concave neck and globular body. From Period IV.
11. Same as above but bigger in size. From Period IV.
12. Fragment of a storage jar of red ware with externally thickened rim, coarse fabric. From Period IV.
13. Vase of red ware with external notches, coarse fabric. From Period IV.
14. Vase of red ware with slightly inturned splayed out rim. From Period IV.
15. Pear-shaped vase of red ware. From Period IV.
16. Vase of red ware with externally thickened rim. From Period IV.

FIG. 11

1. Fragment of a votive tank of red ware. From Period IV.
2. Fragment of a *karāhī*, nail headed rim with uniformly thickened edges. It is distinguished by the presence of a loop on either side. From Period IV.
3. Fragment of a rimless (carinated) *hāndī* with almost a round base. From Period IV.
4. Fragment of a lipped basin of red slipped ware. From Period IV.

FIG. 12

1. Fragment of a bottle-necked vessel of red ware with short, constricted neck and globular profile. From mid phase of Period IV.
2. Fragment of a bottle-necked jar of red ware with a flanged flat rim, narrow neck and bright red slip. The perforation runs through the narrow neck upto the body. From mid phase of Period IV.
3. *Ibid.*
4. A variant of the same with closing mouth and a wider perforation. From Period IV.
5. Fragment of a bottle-necked vessel of red ware with 6 holes in the interior at the shoulder. It has a bright red slip on the exterior. From Period IV.
6. Same as above but with a smaller neck. From Period IV.

7. A variant of the above No. 6 with a pronounced rim edge.
8. *Ibid.*
9. Fragment of a bottle-necked jar of red ware with splayed out rim, narrow neck and globular profile. From Period IV.
10. Fragment, upper part of a sprinkler with obliquely cut flanged rim and a centrally placed conical knob opening. From an early level of Period IV.
11. Fragment, a variant of the above having a longer neck and a centrally placed conical knob opening. It has been treated with bright red slip. The perforation runs through the narrow neck. From mid phase of Period IV.
12. Same as above, differs in having a longer flanged rim and thicker body. From mid phase of Period IV.
13. Fragment of a sprinkler having a flat conical knob opening. The bright red slip on the exterior has now peeled off. From mid phase of Period IV.
14. Variant of the No. 12 but smaller in size. It has been treated with a bright red slip, of fine fabric. From an early level of Period IV.
15. Variant of a sprinkler with flanged edge-rim and centrally placed elongated knobbed opening. From mid phase of Period IV.
16. Fragment of a spout with decoration. From Period IV.
17. Fragment of a spout of a sprinkler. From Period IV.
18. *Ibid.*
19. Fragment of a vase, vertical thickened rim and a long straight narrow neck with grooves on the exterior. From an upper phase of Period IV.
20. Fragment of a finial of red ware, corrugated profile progressively getting wider towards the base. From an upper phase of Period IV.

PERIOD V (GUPTA AND POST-GUPTA DEPOSITS)

The habitational remains of Period V belonged to the Gupta and post-Gupta times. Some walls of the preceding period were used in this period also and two walls measuring 12 m 70 cm (north-south) each, were constructed by reused bricks. An almost square structure of 1.35 x 1.40 m size was constructed in this period for some religious purpose. The structural activity and other finds show that this area was used as a religious complex during this period. Mention may be made of few long ovens (size 4.18, 3.70 and 3.10 m) presumably used as community kitchens on festive/religious occasions (Pl. XIII-A). Extensive damage has been done to the structures of this period by brick robbing in recent years.

The ceramic industry comprises essentially of red ware with some sherds of red polished ware. The principal types in the former include various type of vases and storage jars, inkpot lids, incurved bowls (*parai*) and miniature vessels (Figs. 13-15). The principal shapes are illustrated below:

FIG. 13

1. Fragment of a basin of red ware with nail-headed rim and uniformly thickened sides. It is distinguished by three raised decorations on the top. From Period V.
2. A complete miniature vessel of red ware with externally thickened rim, shallow neck, globular body; medium fabric. From Period V.
3. Complete miniature vessel of red ware with out-turned, externally bevelled rim constricted neck, globular body and a sagger base. From Period V.
4. Fragment of a vase of red ware with out-turned featureless rim, short concave neck, expanding sides, medium fabric. From Period V.
5. Fragment of a vase of red ware with horizontally splayed out rim, concave constricted rim and sides progressively thickened towards base. From Period V.
6. Vase of red ware with externally collared rim, concave neck, two grooves on the exterior at the neck. From Period V.
7. Fragment of a vase of red ware with out-turned collared rim, concave neck and expanding body. From Period V.
8. Vase with out-turned thickened rim, short neck, coarse fabric. From Period V.
9. Fragment of a vase of red ware with splayed out rim, concave neck and expanding body. From Period V.

FIG. 14

1. Fragment of a basin of red ware with externally collared rim and convex sides. From Period V.
2. Fragment of a basin of red ware with inturned collared rim and almost uniformly convex sides. From Period V.
3. Vase of red ware with well thickened internally pressed rim with

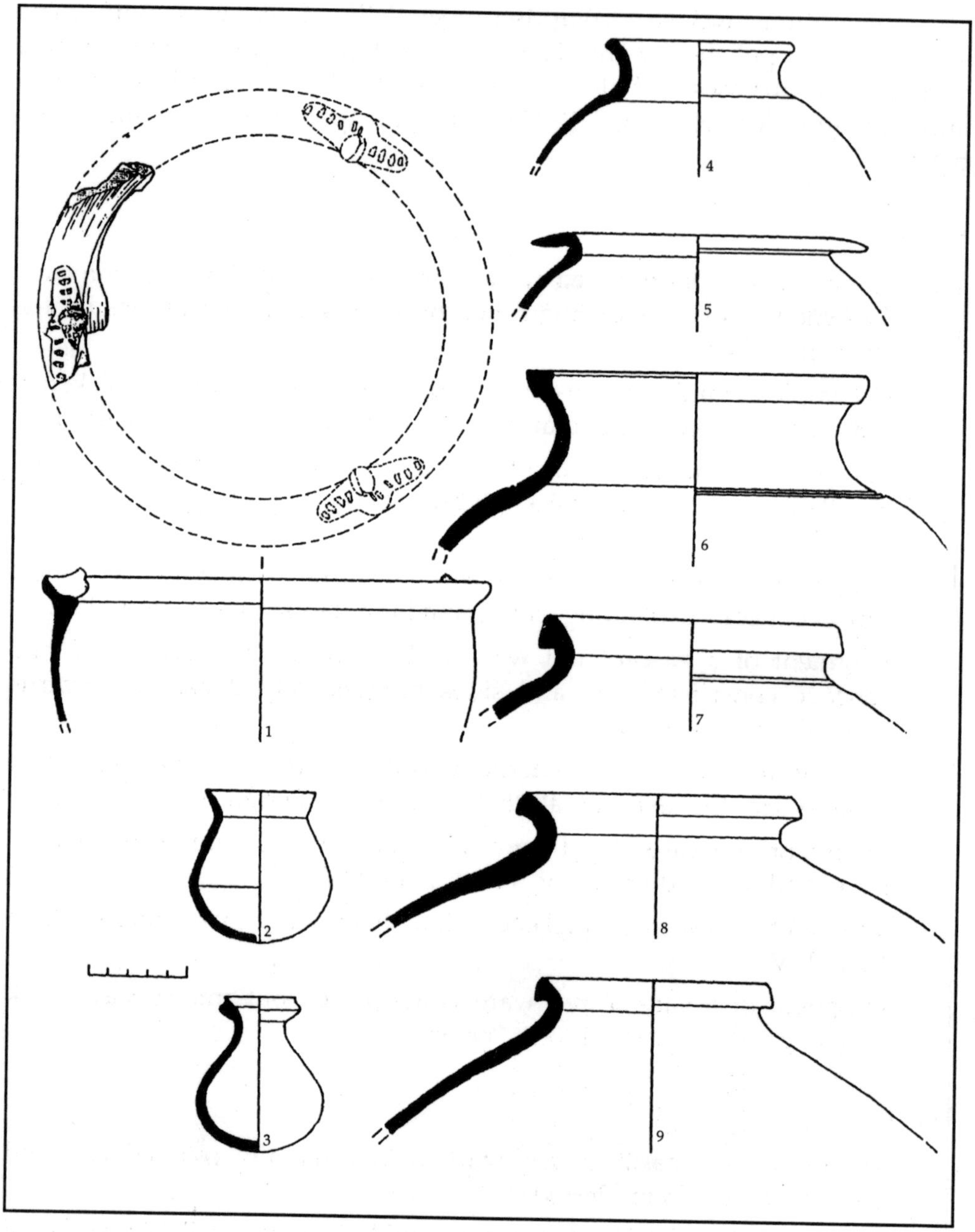

Fig. 13. Red Ware, Period V.

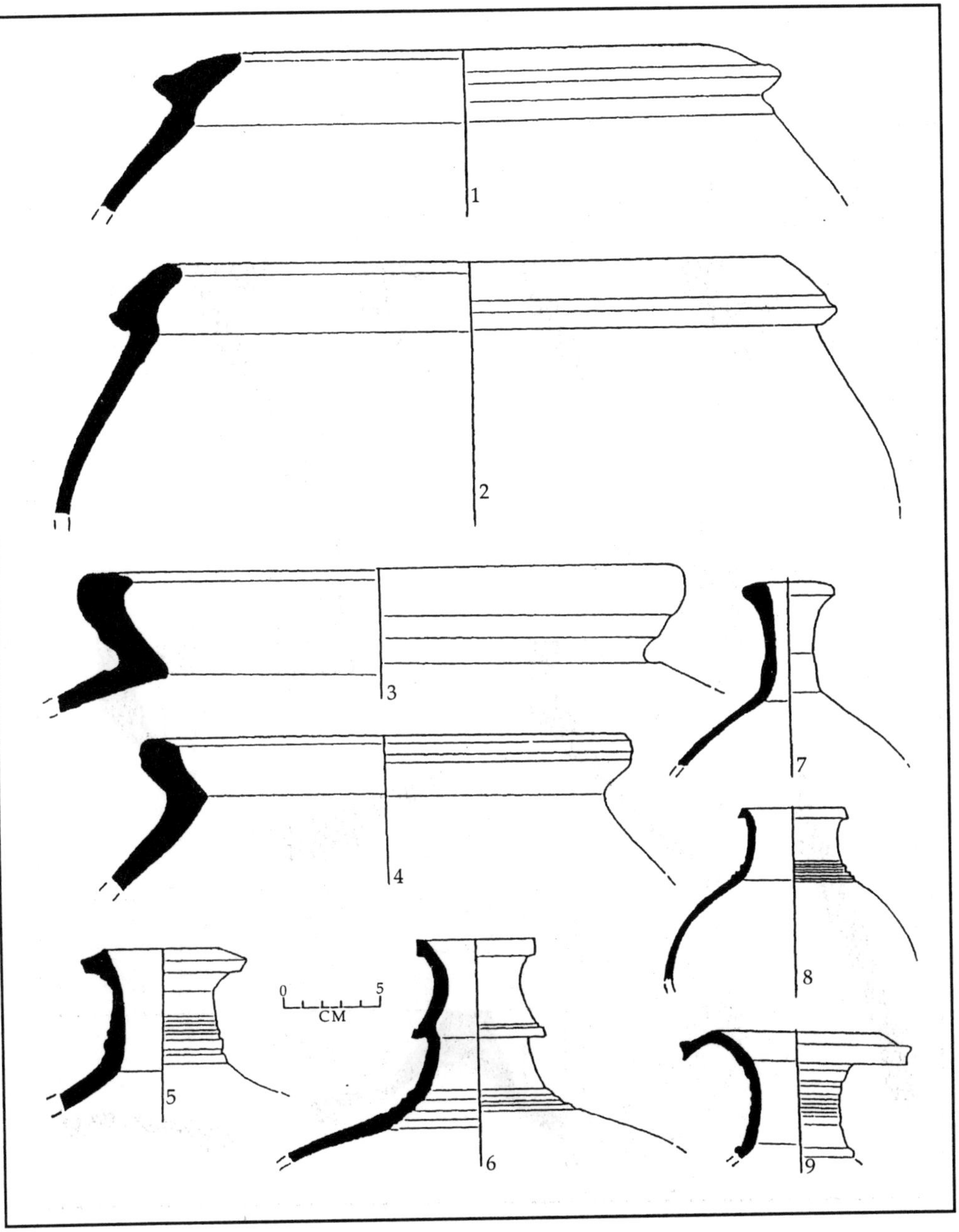

Fig. 14. Red Ware, Period V.

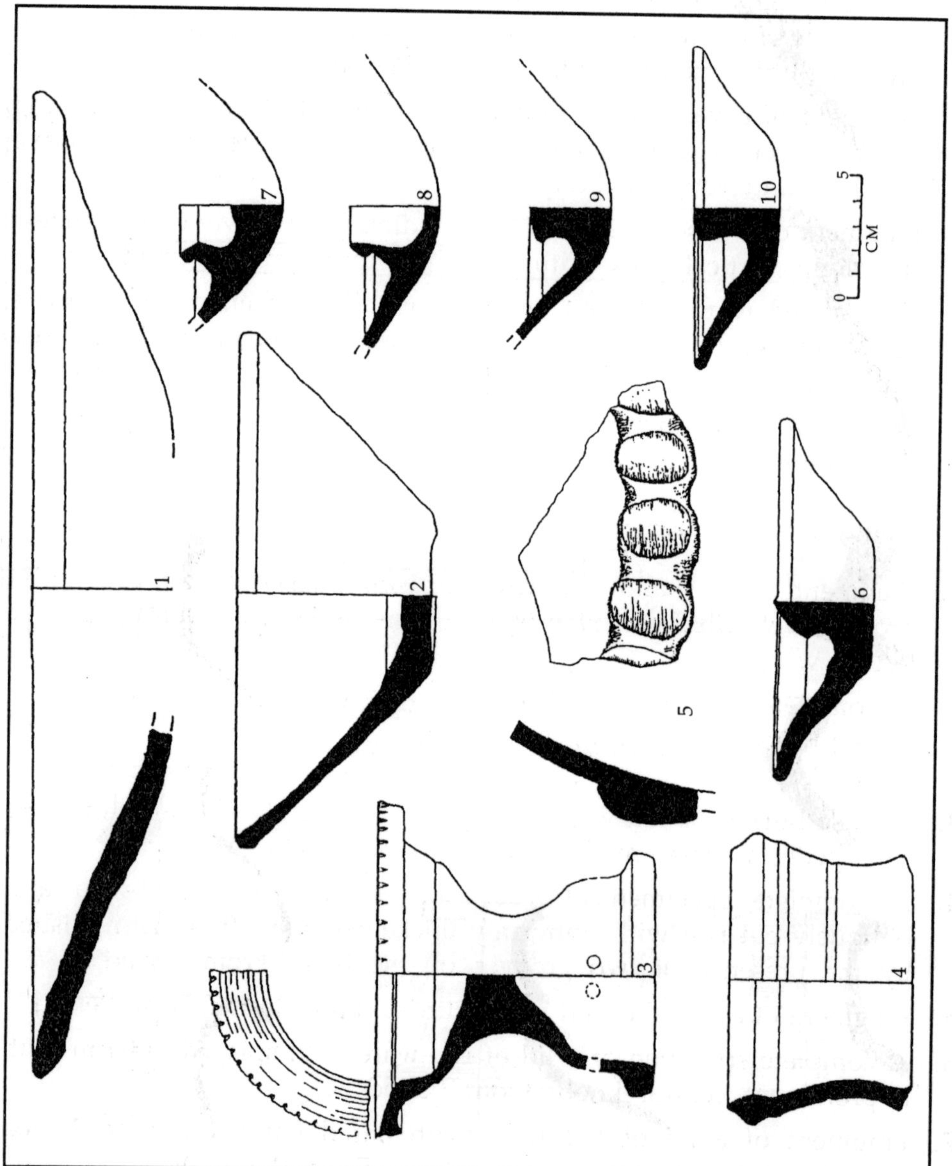

Fig. 15. Red Ware, Period V.

flattish rim top. The body abruptly starts just below the rim which is grooved. From Period V.

4. Same as above with externally thickened rim. From Period V.
5. Fragment of a vessel of red ware with externally clubbed rim, an expanding mouth, almost vertical externally grooved neck with prominent ribs in the middle. From Period V.
6. Fragment of a vase of red slipped ware with featureless rim, a long concave neck with bold midrib, prominent carinated short concave shoulder and rounded body. From upper level of Period V.
7. Fragment of a vase of red ware, expanding mouth, everted featureless rim, long vertical neck with globular profile. From Period V.
8. Vase of red ware with out-turned externally thickened rim, concave neck and expanding shoulders which are grooved; treated with red slip which is peeled off at places. From upper level of Period V.
9. Vase of red ware with out-turned thickened rim, constricted neck. From Period V.

FIG. 15

1. Fragment of a shallow plate-cum-basin, thickened rim and sides progressively thicker towards flat base. From an upper phase of Period V.
2. A complete specimen of a bowl of red ware with featureless rim, sides progressively thicker towards a thick flat base, medium fabric. From Period V.
3. Incense burner of red ware with horizontally splayed out featureless rim, pedestal base, medium fabric. From Period V.
4. A complete specimen of a stand, externally thickened rim and obliquely cut rim with uniformly thickened sides. It is distinguished by the presence of two grooves on the body. From Period V.
5. Fragment of a vessel of red ware with appliqué design. From Period V.
6. A complete specimen of a lid of red ware with splayed out rim with a prominent central knob. From Period V.
7. Fragment of a lid of red ware with flared flat waist, vase-shaped central depression and a sagger base. From Period V.
8. *Ibid.*
9. Fragment of a lid of red ware with extremely flared rim and a sagger base. From Period V.

10. Same as above but with a almost straight knob. From Period V.

Fragments of stone jambs of temples with *Krishna-Lila* scenes carved on them and broken sculptures of Ambika, Ganesha, Surya and Ek Mukh Shivalinga datable to tenth-twelfth centuries AD are lying on the present-day temple of Lutabir located south-west of present Agiabir village (Singh, 2001 : 201-205).

Besides, two test pits measuring 2 m x 2 m size respectively were excavated on Mound-3 located ½ km east from the main mound. Remains of late phase of NBPW were noticed in the lower level of these trenches. This site continued to be inhabited till the Gupta period.

3

Metal Objects

The excavation yielded limited number of copper objects but the site was rich in iron antiquities. The spectacular discovery of a cache of copper and iron objects from Period III is an important discovery.

COPPER

Copper objects are unfortunately not many but the presence of this metal in Period I has been registered by a single fish-hook. Four copper objects were recovered from Period II but their number suddenly increases in Period III. As many as 20 specimens including 10 vessels, wires, antimony rods, bangles, earrings, pendant, etc., have been recorded from this period. The periodwise distribution of these antiquities is given in the Table 3.1.

IRON

As compared to copper antiquities, the collection of iron objects is impressive indeed. Iron objects appear in significant number in Period II which has yielded 35 objects. These comprise 6 nails, 6 chisels, two knives, one arrowhead and 20 objects of indeterminate use. This figure has doubled in Period III where we have 73 specimens comprising of 15 nails, 12 chisels, 5 knives, 8 spearheads, 2 swords, 1 lampstand and 28 objects of indeterminate use. The number of iron objects in Periods IV and V dwindled down to 18 and 5 pieces respectively mainly because the cultural strata of these two periods were disturbed and robbed by the villagers.

The distribution of iron objects is as in Table 3.2.

TABLE 3.1

Object	Period I	Period II	Period III	Period IV	Period V	Total
1. Antimony Rod	-	01	04	02	01	08
2. Bangle	-	-	01	-	-	01
3. Earring	-	-	01	-	-	01
4. Fish-hook	01	-	-	-	-	01
5. Indeterminate	-	01	-	02	01	04
6. Pendant	-	-	01	-	-	01
7. Ring	-	01	01	01	-	03
8. Wire	-	01	02	-	-	03
9. Vessel	-	-	-	-	-	-
(a) Bowl	-	-	02	-	-	02
(b) Carinated *Hāndī*	-	-	02	-	-	02
(c) *Hāndā*	-	-	03	-	-	03
(d) *Lota*	-	-	01	-	-	01
(e) Knobbed Vessel	-	-	01	-	-	01
(f) Mirror	-	-	01	-	-	01
TOTAL	**01**	**04**	**20**	**05**	**02**	**32**

TABLE 3.2

Type	Period I	Period II	Period III	Period IV	Period V	Total
1. Arrowhead	-	01	01	01	-	03
2. Chisel	-	06	12	02	-	20
3. Knife	-	02	05	01	-	08
4. Lampstand	-	-	01	-	-	01
5. Miniature Pot	-	-	01	-	-	01
6. Nail	-	06	15	03	03	27
7. Ring	-	-	-	01	-	01
8. Spearhead	-	-	08	02	01	11
9. Sword	-	-	02	-	-	02
10. Indeterminate	-	20	28	08	01	57
TOTAL	**-**	**35**	**73**	**18**	**05**	**131**

During the 2000-2001 excavations, the most important discovery of Period III was a cache of copper and iron objects found in a room (Singh and Singh, 2001; 109-115) (Pl. XIV-B). This cache was buried in layer (12) and was resting on the top of layer (13) which represents a rammed clay floor (Fig. 4). The copper objects *in situ* include three vases (*hāndās*) with flaring rim and body diameters of 41, 37.6 and 35 cm respectively, two carinated *hāndīs* with featureless rims and body diameters of 31 and 30.8 cm respectively, one lid-like object (knobbed vessel), one *lota*-shaped vessel with diameter at the mouth of 27.6 cm), one bowl with incurved rim and diameter at the mouth of 15.1 cm, one miniature bowl with featureless rim and diameter at the mouth of 11 cm and a mirror. All these objects except the *lota* were placed upside down at a depth of 6.60 m below datum (Pl. XIV-B). The iron objects include two swords with lengths of 69.5 and 64.5 cm respectively and a lampstand. A bowl with four raised dots at the rim is fitted on its top and a circular shallow plate is fitted just below. Such a cache of vessels and implements has not been reported so far from any other NBPW site.

CULTURAL CONTEXT

As stated above, the cache was found buried in layer (12) and was resting on the top of layer (13) which represents a rammed clay floor. The contents of these two layers comprise coarse grey ware and a coarser variety of NBP. The frequency of black slipped ware is less. Bowls and dishes of black slipped and grey ware have either a pointed knob in the centre or concentric circles with a raised knob in the centre. These pottery types were recorded from Period IC at Rajghat (Narain & Roy 1977, Fig. 10, No. 2-5) and Period II at Sarai Mohana (personal observation of the second author). Besides, certain new types of vessels occur in red ware.These comprise pear-shaped vase with several variants (Ahichchhatra 10A), vases and miniature vessels, carinated *hāndī* with featureless rim, bowls with flat base and dishes with sagger base. All these pottery shapes occur in the time bracket of 300-400 BC on several sites in the Ganga Valley. The antiquities recovered from these layers are antimony rods and beads of copper, together with iron objects, bone points, beads of semi-precious stones, balls and skin rubbers of terracotta. Two silos were also exposed in the vicinity of this cache in the northern and south-eastern sides of the house. A uniform burning of 20 cm at the base of layer (13) was noticed throughout the excavated area of 5.15 m x 2.50 m. As the excavation was confined to a small area, it is difficult to determine whether this burning is deliberate or accidental and whether it is local to this part of the habitation site or is a part of general conflagration of the site by invaders. A similar burning activity of the same period was noticed in the corresponding levels at Narhan (Singh 1994 : 14) and Jhusi (personal observation). A detailed account of the objects found in this cache is given below :

Fig. 16; (Pl. XVI-A) A complete cooking vessel (*hāndā*) of copper with flaring, featureless rim, constricted neck, carinated shoulder, expanding sides and a sagger base. The bottom surface of the pot is rough and burnt. This hammered copper pot was made in two pieces, riveted together at the shoulder.

Diameter of the mouth	:	24.7 cm
Diameter of the body	:	41 cm
Thickness of the rim	:	0.50 cm
Height of the vessel	:	39.6 cm

ABR / 2000-2001, Trench-YE6 III-IV, Stratum (13) Depth-6.60 m

Fig. 17; (Pl. XVI-B) A complete cooking vessel (*hāndā*) of copper with flaring, featureless rim, constricted neck, carinated shoulder, slightly expanding sides and a sagger base. The bottom surface of the pot is blackish and burnt.

Diameter of the mouth	:	20.2 cm
Diameter of the body	:	37.6 cm
Thickness of the rim	:	0.53 cm
Height of the vessel	:	36.6 cm

ABR / 2000-2001, Trench-YE6 III-IV, Stratum (13) Depth-6.60 m

Fig. 18; (Pl. XVII-A) A complete vase (*hāndā*) of copper with flaring, featureless rim, constricted neck, carinated shoulder, slightly expanding sides and a sagger base. The bottom surface of the pot is blackish and burnt.

Diameter of the mouth	:	21 cm
Diameter of the body	:	35 cm
Thickness of the rim	:	0.52 cm
Height of the vessel	:	34 cm

ABR / 2000-2001, Trench-YE6 III-IV, Stratum (13) Depth-6.60 m

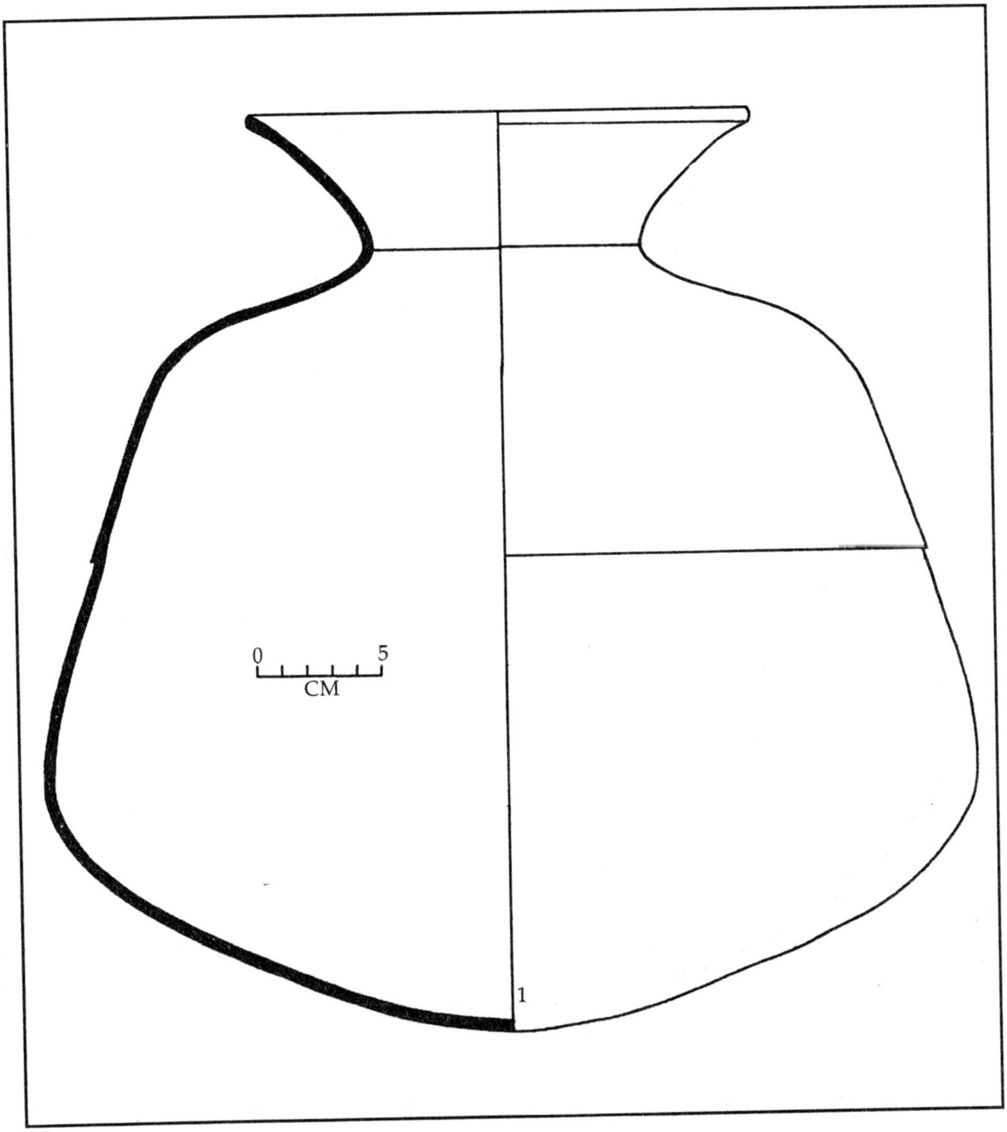

Fig. 16. Cooking vessel (*Hāndā*) of copper, Period III.

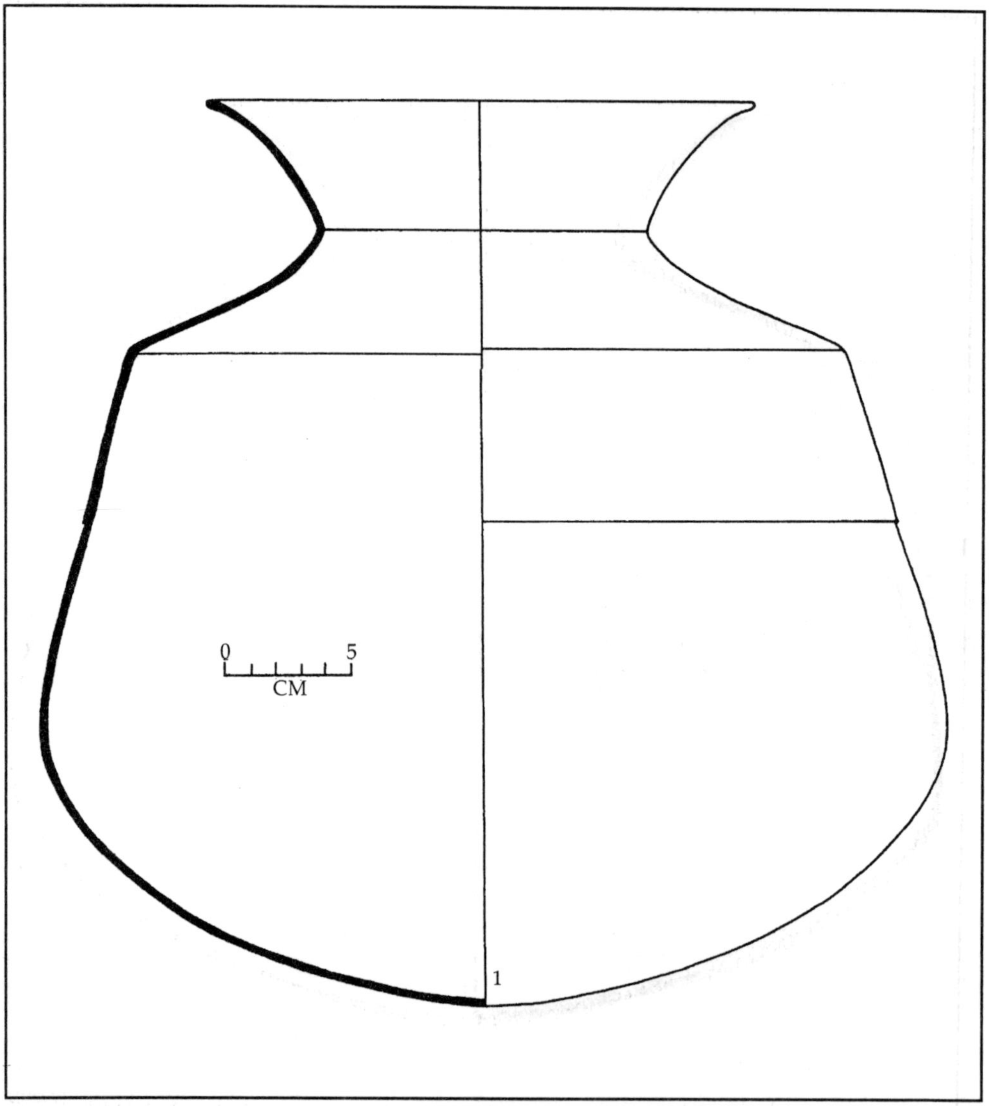

Fig. 17. Cooking vessel (*Hāndā*) of copper, Period III.

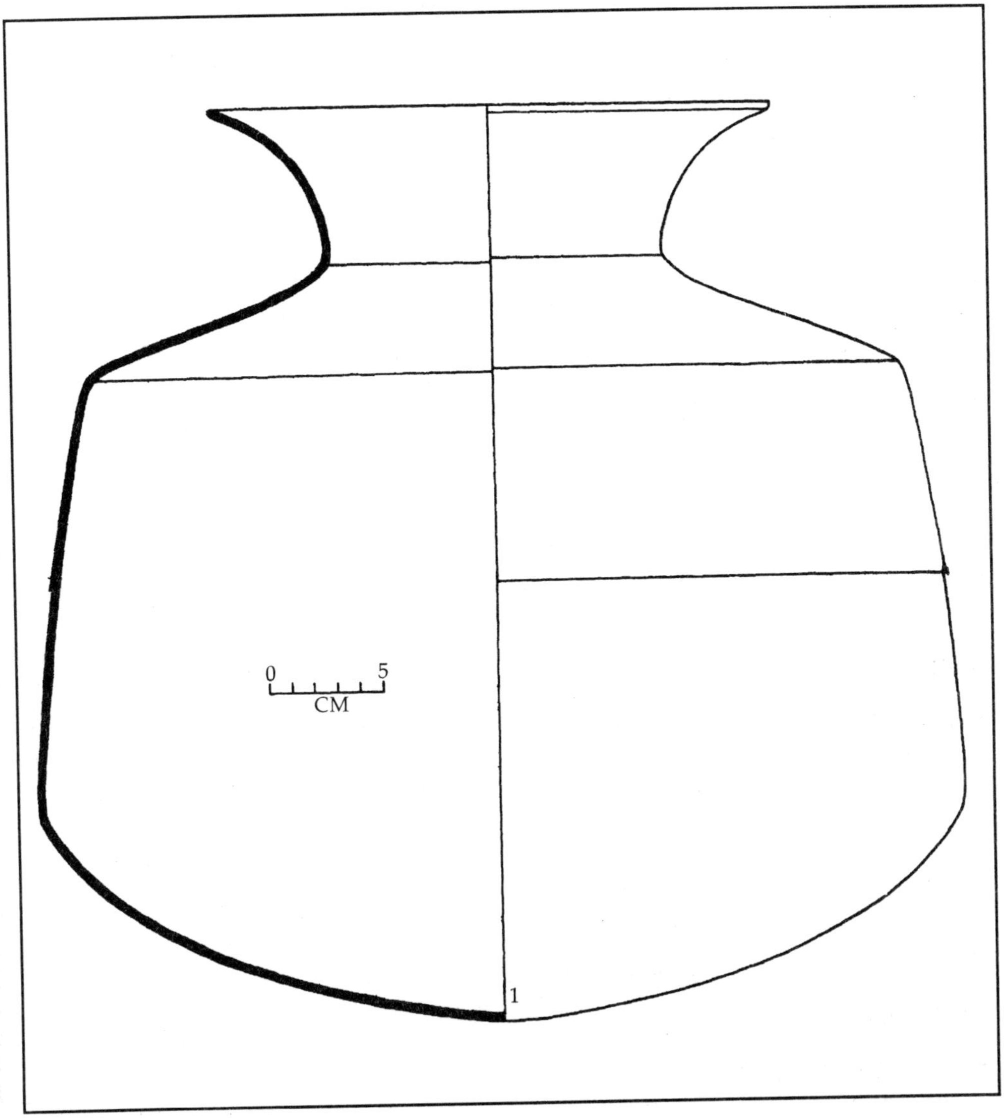

Fig. 18. Cooking vessel (*Hāndā*) of copper, Period III.

Fig. 19. No. 1. (Pl. XV-A) A complete miniature bowl of copper with internally bevelled rim, convex sides.

Diameter of the mouth	:	11 cm
Thickness of the rim	:	0.71 cm
Height of the bowl	:	5.4 cm

ABR / 2000-2001, Trench-YE6 III-IV, Stratum (13) Depth-6.60 m

No. 2; (Pl. XV-B) A complete bowl of copper with featureless rim edge, uniformly thin sides with footed base.

Diameter of the mouth	:	15.1 cm
Thickness of the rim	:	0.40 cm
Height of the bowl	:	5.2 cm

ABR / 2000-2001, Trench-YE6 III-IV, Stratum (13) Depth-6.60 m

No.3; (Pl. XVII-B) A complete specimen of *lota*, out-turned thickened rim, high concave neck, globular body and flat base.

Diameter of the mouth	:	10.5 cm
Diameter of the body	:	15.5 cm
Thickness of the rim	:	0.58 cm
Height of the *lota*	:	17.2 cm

ABR / 2000-2001, Trench-YE6 III-IV, Stratum (13) Depth-6.60 m

No. 4; (Pl. XVIII-A) A complete carinated (rimless) *hāndī* of copper with featureless rim. In this case the rim is pressed inside the pot.

Diameter of the mouth	:	19 cm
Diameter of the body	:	30.8 cm
Thickness of the rim	:	0.28 cm
Height of the vessel	:	9.09 cm

ABR / 2000-2001, Trench-YE6 III-IV, Stratum (13) Depth-6.60 m

No. 5; (Pl. XVIII-B) A complete carinated (rimless) *hāndī* of copper with closing featureless rim and almost a round base.

Diameter of the mouth	:	19 cm
Diameter of the body	:	31 cm
Thickness of the rim	:	0.30 cm
Height of the vessel	:	9 cm

Pl. XVIIA. Cooking vessel (*Hāndā*) of copper, Period III.

Pl. XVIIB. *Lota* of copper, Period III.

Pl. XVIIIA. Carinated *Hāndī* of copper, Period III.

Pl. XVIIIB. Carinated *Hāndī* of copper, Period III.

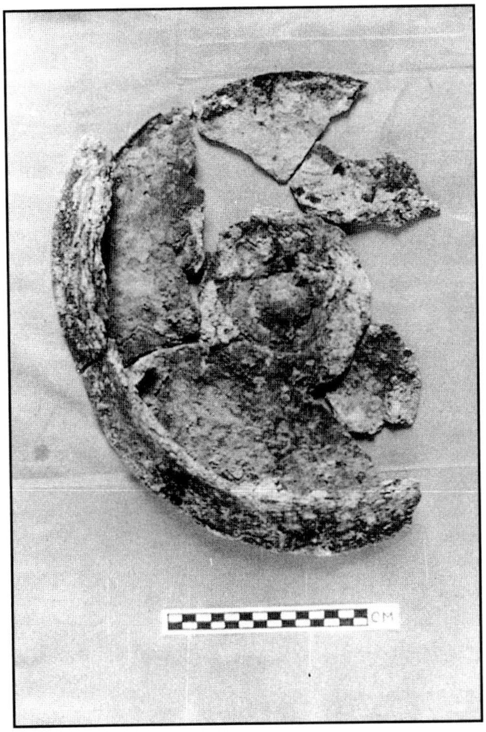

Pl. XIXA. Knobbed lid of copper, Period III.

Pl. XIXB. Copper mirror, Period III.

Pl. XXA. Iron swords, Period III.

Pl. XXB. Iron lampstand, Period III.

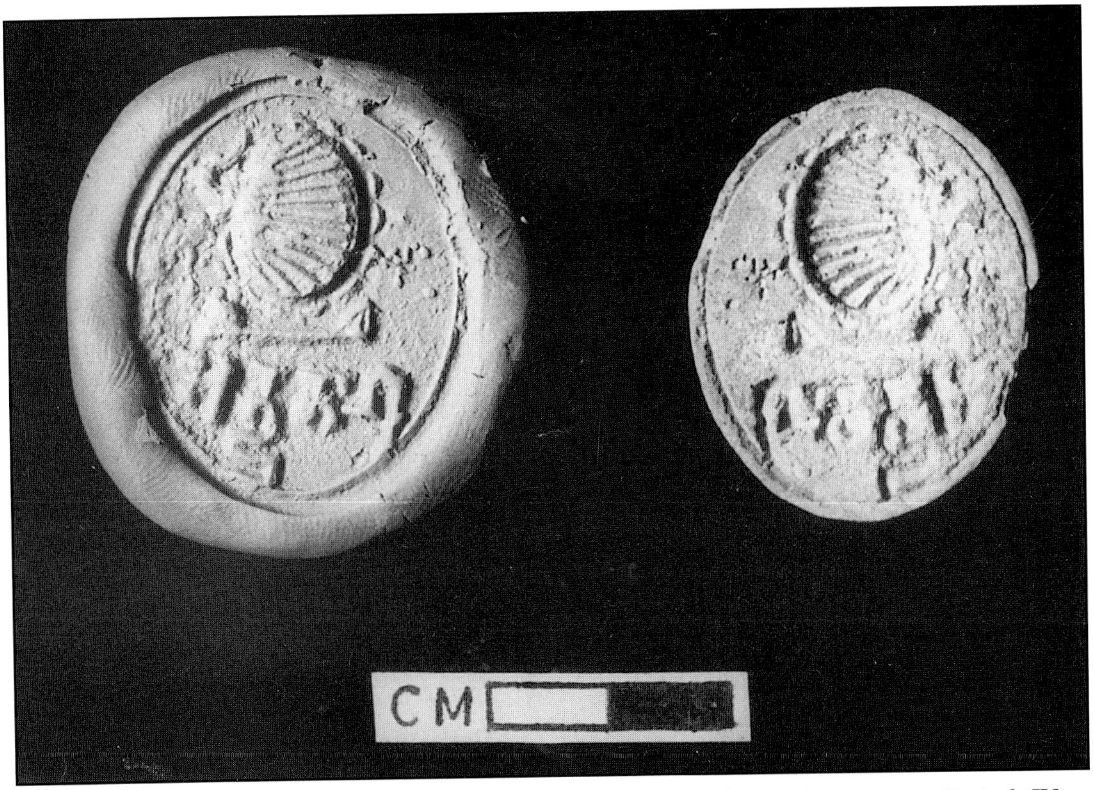

Pl. XXIA. An ivory seal with legend 'Skandanaga' and its plaster cast, Period IV.

Pl. XXIB. Sealing of baked clay with legend 'Harisenasya' and its reverse, Period IV.

Pl. XXIIA. Sealing of baked clay with legend 'Rudrapalasya' and with symbols, ▲ and other sealings.

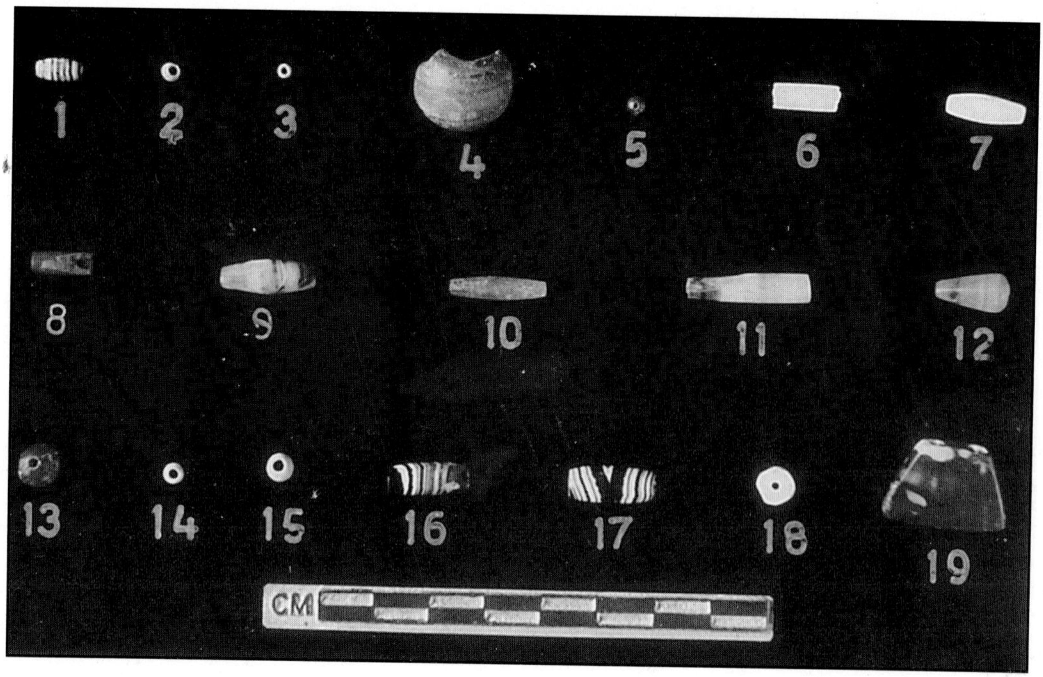

Pl. XXIIB. Beads of semi-precious stones, Periods I & II.

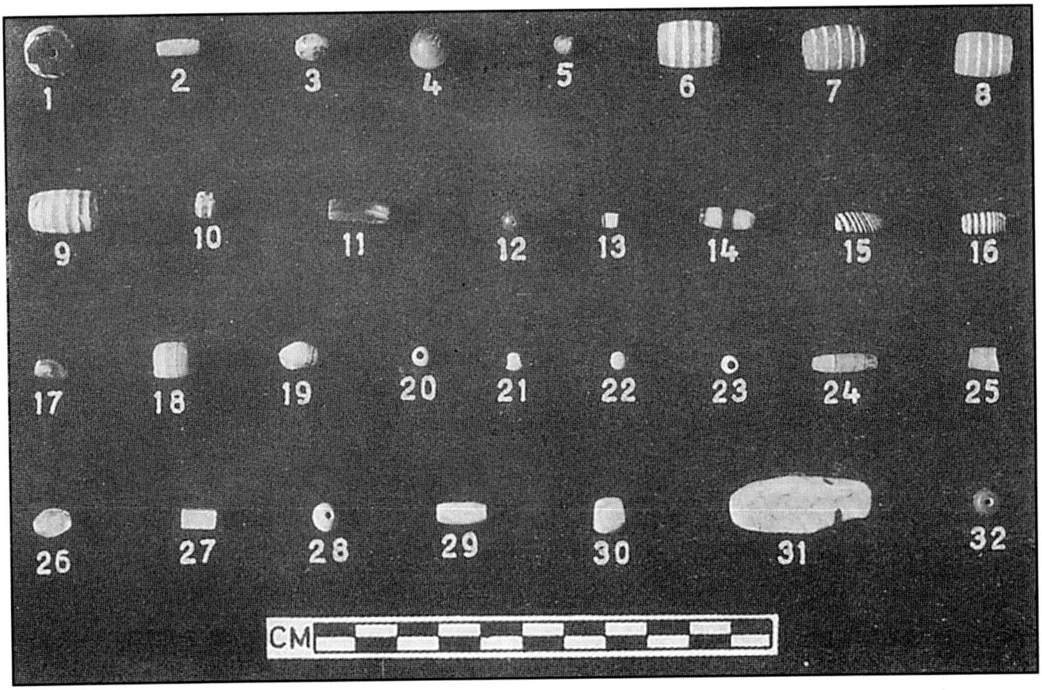

Pl. XXIIIA. Beads of semi-precious stones, Periods III & IV.

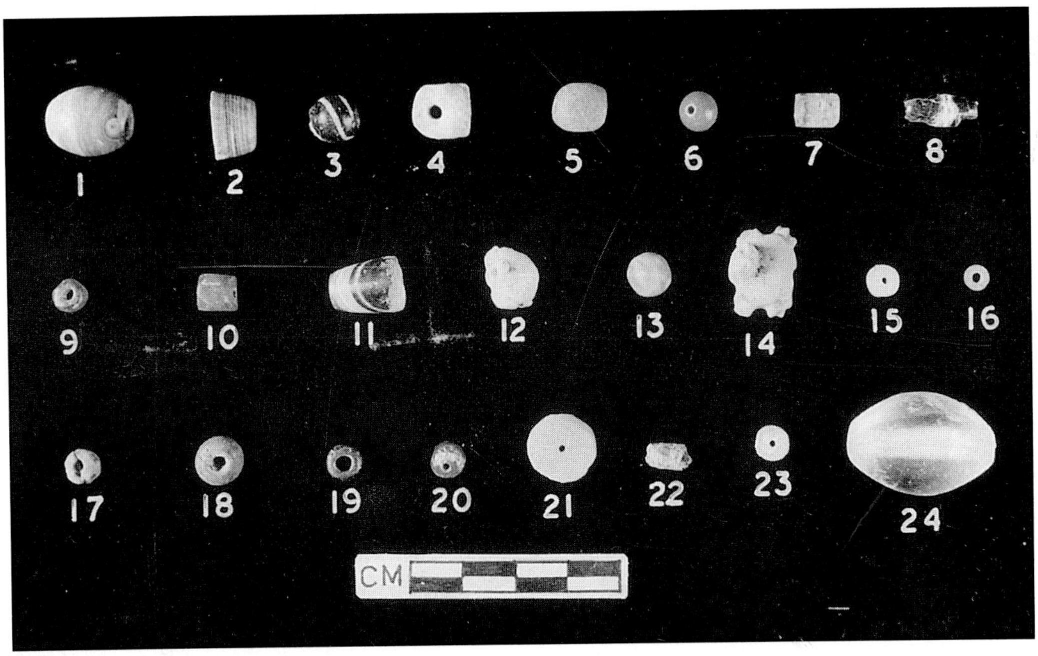

Pl. XXIIIB. Beads of semi-precious stones, Periods IV & V.

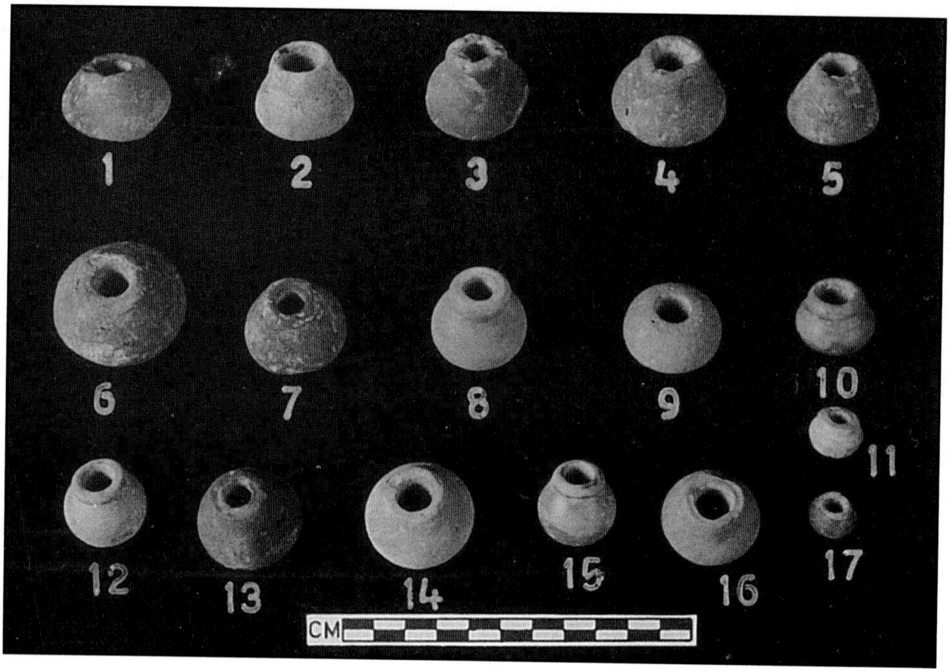

Pl. XXIVA. Terracotta beads of Periods I & II.

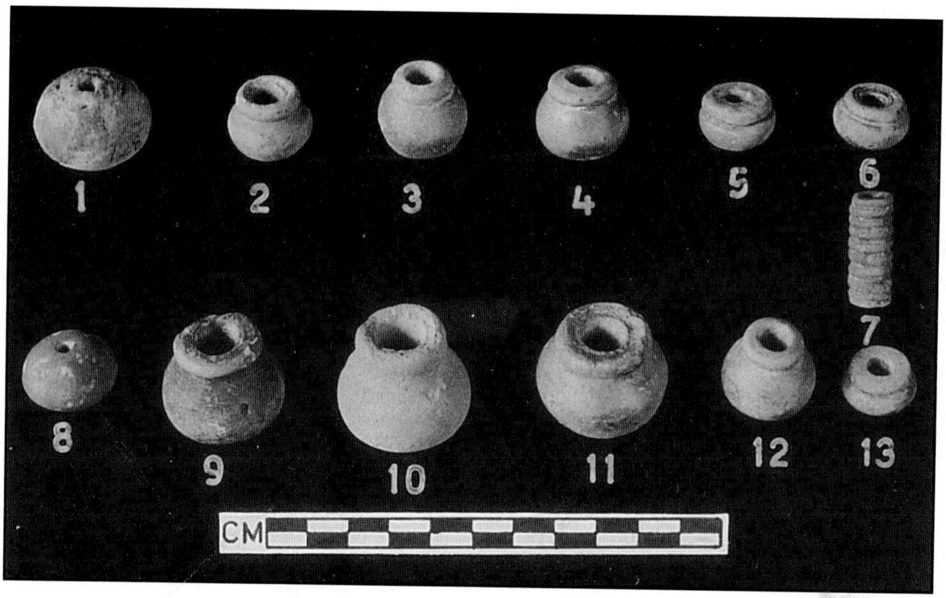

Pl. XXIVB. Terracotta beads of Periods III & IV.

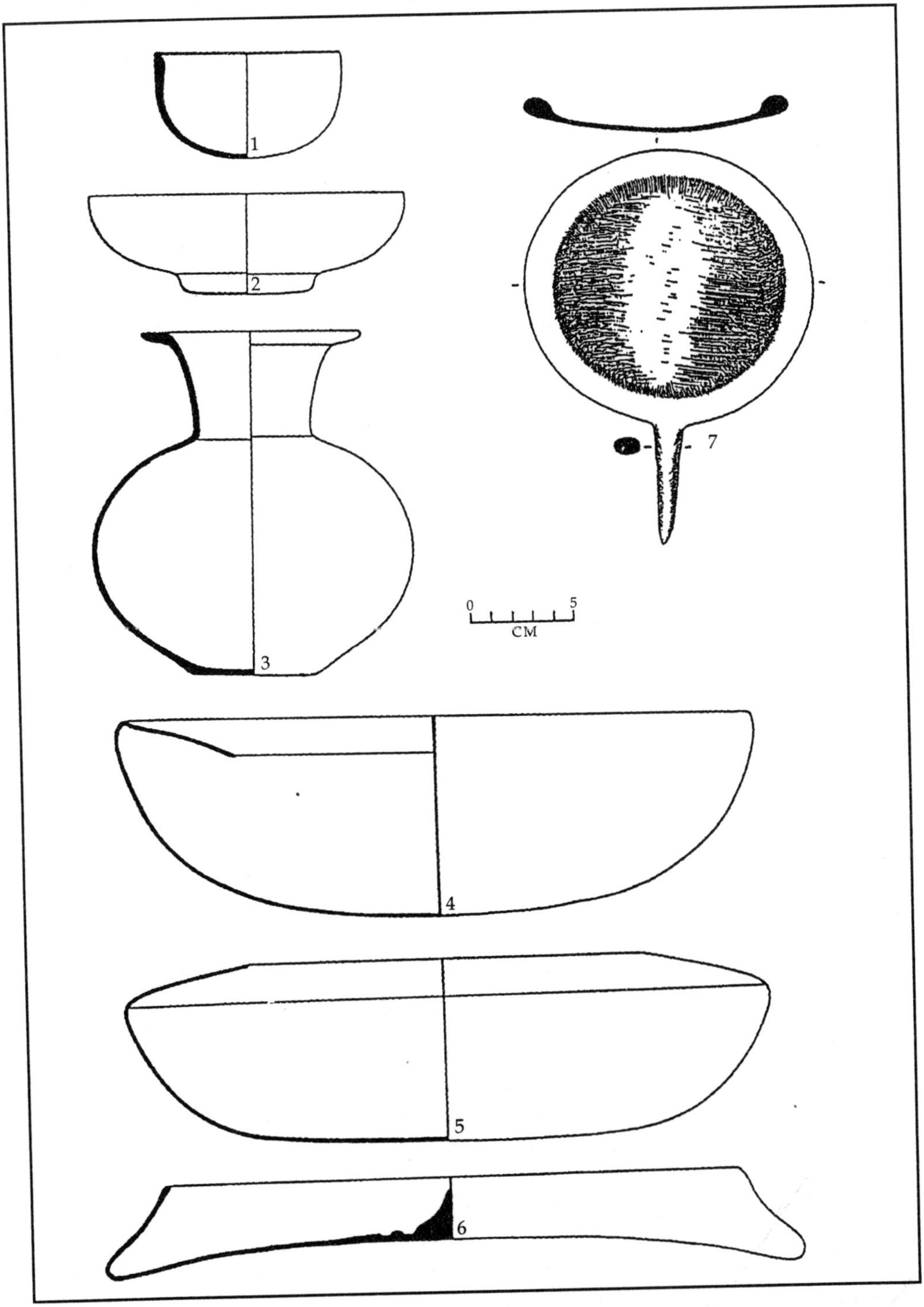

Fig. 19. Copper vessels and mirror, Period III.

ABR / 2000-2001, Trench-YE6 III-IV, Stratum (13) Depth-6.60 m

Similar carinated (rimless) *hāndī* of copper occurs at Narhan, district Gorakhpur from the earliest phase of NBPW (Singh 1994 : Pl. XX-C).

No. 6; (Pl. XIX-A) Lid of copper with short incurved closing rim, flattened from the top and a slightly concave base. It has a pointed solid knob on the inner side of the base with one concentric raised band around it. Similar concentric raised bands are present in the bowls of Rajghat in Period IC (Narain & Roy 1977 : fig. 10, Nos. 2-5).

Diameter of the mouth	:	27.6 cm
Diameter of the body	:	33.6 cm
Thickness of the rim	:	0.57 cm
Height of the vessel	:	3.2 cm

ABR / 2000-2001, Trench-YE6 III-IV, Stratum (13) Depth-6.60 m

No. 7; (Pl. XIX-B) A complete copper mirror, broad, circular in outline, thick rim edge and a pointed handle. The face of the mirror is smooth and slightly convex. The back portion of the mirror is plain.

Diameter of the mirror	:	14 cm
Thickness of the rim	:	1 cm
Length of the mirror (including the tang)	:	20 cm
Length of the handle	:	6 cm

ABR / 2000-2001, Trench-YE6 III-IV, Stratum (13) Depth-6.60 m

Two copper mirrors are reported from the Mason Dih, district-Ghazipur (about 60 km. north-east of Agiabir) in the NBPW levels and the other having a handle and a hook in the Gupta levels respectively (*IAR* 1964-65 : 42-43; Ghosh, 1989, Vol. I : 348).

Fig. 20. No. 1. A complete double edged sword of iron with thin blade,

(Pl. XX-A) pointed tip, solid tang of circular cross-section, highly encrusted.

Length of the blade	:	69.5 cm

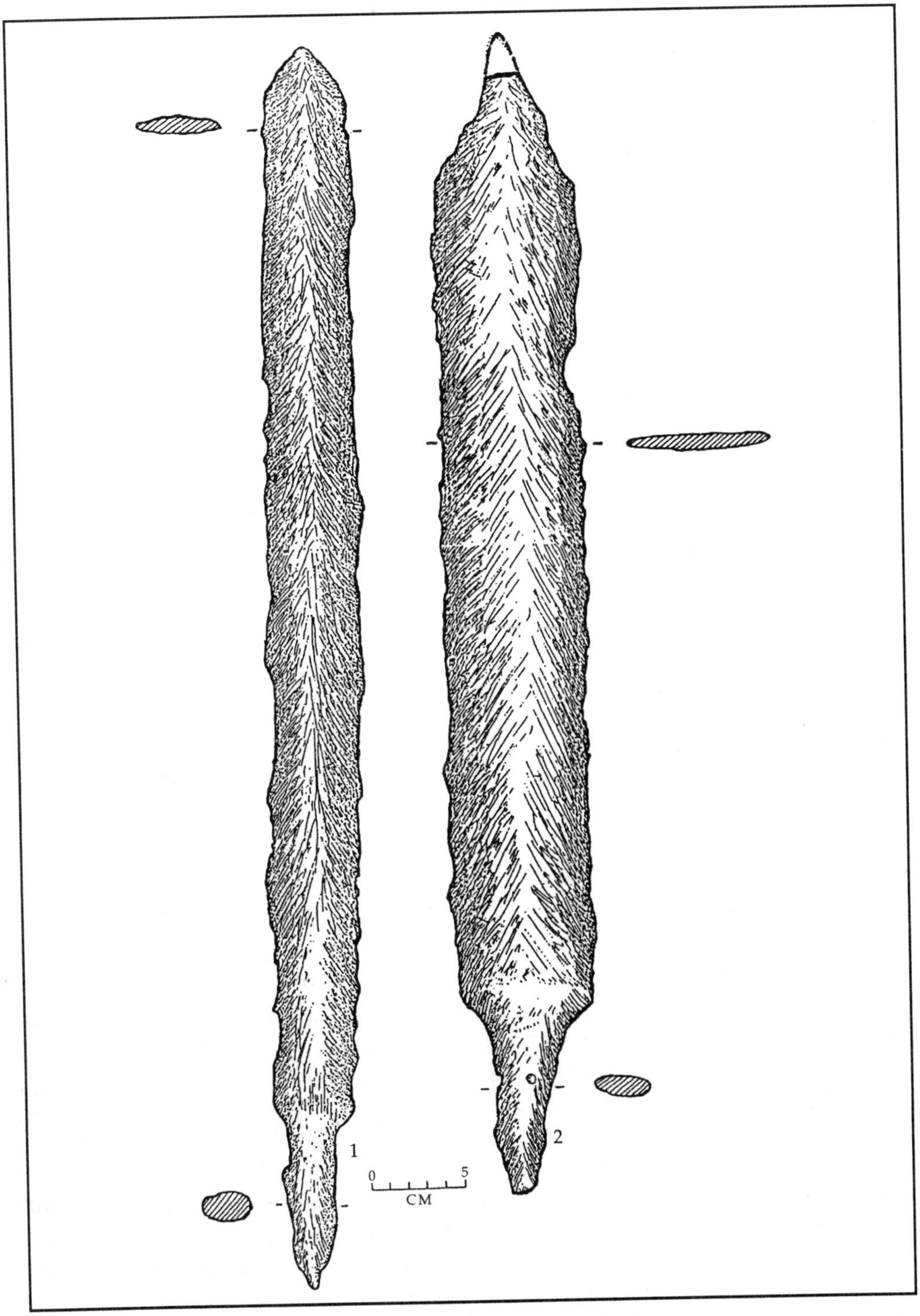

Fig. 20. Iron swords, Period III.

	Width of the blade	:	5.30 cm
	Length of the tang	:	10 cm
No. 2.	Double edged sword of iron with thin blade, edges tapering to a pointed tip, solid tang of circular cross-section, badly corrugated.		
	Length of the blade	:	64.5 cm
	Width of the blade	:	8 cm
	Length of the tang	:	10 cm
Fig. 21; (Pl.XX-B)	Lampstand		
	Length of the Lampstand	:	1.07 m
	Thickness of the Rod	:	4 cm
	Diameter of the base	:	43 cm
	Diameter of the bowl (fitted on the top of the lampstand)	:	14 cm
	Diameter of the shallow plate (fitted below the above bowl)	:	24 cm

Identical cooking vessels of copper have been recovered from the Saka-Parthian city of Sirkap and have been dated to 1st century AD (Marshall, 1951: 258, Pl. 174, Nos. 257-258). A copper vessel of similar type was also reported from Chandraketugarh (district-24 Parganas, West Bengal) from surface (Ghosh 1989 : 95-96) and another vessel was found from Mahasthangarh (Bangladesh) from the Kushana levels. An identical example comes from the NBPW level at Narhan (Singh 1994, Pl. XX-C).

Circular mirrors polished on one side and plain or decorated on the other, have been found in limited number at several sites. Two copper mirrors with a long tang are reported from Harappa (Vats 1940: 391). The diameter of these mirrors are 16 cm and 17.50 cm respectively. The finest examples of copper mirrors (nineteen in number) come from Taxila, where they were found in the Saka-Parthian levels at Sirkap datable to 1st century BC-AD(Marshall, 1951: 215: 584-85, Pl. 182, Nos. 208-211).They are circular in shape and vary between 5.55 and 16.5 cm in diameter. Three specimens have been found in the Kundangar Hoard at Brahmapuri (district-Kolhapur) placed in a large metal pot buried in a room of the Satavahana period (1st-3rd centuries AD) (Khandalavala 1960 : 27-95). Two copper mirrors were reported from Mason Dih (district Ghazipur, UP), one in the NBPW levels and the other in the Gupta levels (*IAR* 1964-65: 42-43; Ghosh 1989, Vol. I : 348). Two handled circular bronze mirrors

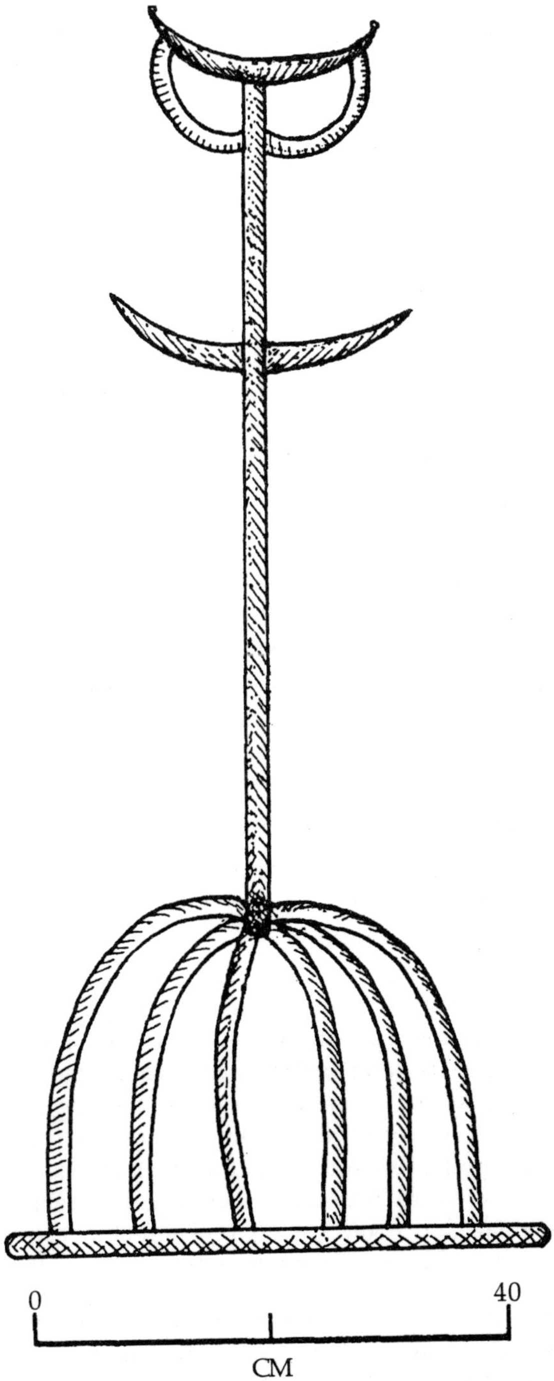

Fig. 21. Lamp stand of iron, Period III.

with recessed face have been reported from Rairh (Puri, 1998 : 43; Pl. XXI, No. 14). Similar knobbed vessels were recovered from Wari-Bateswar region of district Narshingdi (Bangladesh) (Pathan, 1989; Basa *et al.*, 1998) and Bon Don Ta Phet (Thailand) (Rajpitak *et al.*, 1979 : 26-31).

As regards the swords, identical iron swords found at Taxila vary from 52 to 85 cm in length and belong to 1st century AD. Strabo and Arrian state that in fourth century BC the Indian soldiers carried broad swords three cubits in length (Marshall 1951, Vol. II: 542-43, Pl. 164). Iron lampstands of this size are not reported from any site in India. The two lampstands (*candelabra*) recovered from Taxila have been dated to the 1st century AD (Marshall 1951, Vol. II : 542). These consist of a plain vertical rod with a tripod base and leaf like terminal or ring at the top. The height of these lamps varies from 52 cm to one metre (Marshall 1951 : 542, Pl. 163, Nos. 33-35). From the above description it is clear that cooking vessels, swords and lampstands occurring at other sites belong to a much later date than those from Agiabir.

The chemical analysis of carinated *hāndīs* of Agiabir and Narhan and knobbed vessel of Agiabir was done by P.K. Chattopadhyay (Singh & Chattopadhyaya, 2002 : 101-106).The result shows that these were made of high tin bronze. Similar high tin bronze vessels were recovered from Chadraketugarh (West Bengal) and Mahasthangarh (Bangladesh) and Ban Don Ta Phet (Thailand). These evidences may be suggestive of contacts between India and South-East Asia. Whether there were technological and cultural contacts between these two regions need to be studied further.

Chemical analysis of samples from the knobbed vessel of Agiabir and carinated *hāndīs* of Narhan and Agiabir was done by P.K. Chattopadhyay whose observations are as follows:

> Visually the surfaces of the three specimens were observed through a microscope. The carinated bowl from Agiabir (Sp. No. 1) was clean at its internal surface but it was found with soot marks at its outer surface with a coating of clay and ash. One may observe, the use of clay at the outer surface of the cooking pots is done in villages even today. This clay layer protects the vessel from the soots produced in the fire of woods. The application of this protecting clay layer indicates the use of the same tradition for thousands of years. The outer surfaces of all these three objects were found fully converted into malachite [$CuCO_3$. $Cu(OH)_2$] and other complex minerals. In case of copper-bronze objects this is a common feature (Chase 1979).

Chemical analyses of the three specimens was made to identify the constituents and alloying, if any, with the help of Atomic Absorption Spectrophotometer (Perkin Elmer 238).

ANALYSIS OF OBJECTS

The first analysis of the copper objects from Narhan done by R.N. Singh *et al.* had thrown a new light on the initiation of copper technology at this site (Singh, Meprkel and Singh, 1996-97). Analysis of fish-hook and bangle from Period I and bead of Period III clearly indicates that there is no evidence of using pure copper for manufacturing artefacts whereas use of alloy were recorded as low tin bronzes with the addition of tin from 3.806 to 9.857 per cent. They conducted these analyses in University College, London with SEM and EPMA. In the contemporary copper bronzes of Bihar and West Bengal similar observations were recorded with Emission Spectrograph where evidences of tin were found around 10 per cent (Chattopadhyay, 1992). The results obtained by Chattopadhyay are shown in the following Table 3.3.

TABLE 3.3

No.	*Site/ Vessel*	*Cu*	*Sn*	*Ag*	*Pb*	*Fe*	*Zn*
1.	Agiabir / (Carinated *hāndī*)	98.50	>0.1	0.02	>0.1	>0.1	>0.1
2.	Narhan / (Carinated *hāndī*)	99.02	>0.1	0.005	>0.1	>0.1	>0.1
3.	Agiabir (Knobbed Vessel)	35.83	17.98	0.02	>0.1	>0.1	N.T.

The specimen numbers 1 and 2 from the above table clearly indicate that there is no evidence of alloying in the two carinated vessels from Agiabir and Narhan. The specimen No. 3, the knobbed vessel of Agiabir, was specifically searched more precisely for copper, tin, lead and zinc. The oxidized contents, i.e. non-metallic constituents discouraged the cent per cent analysis. The ratio in metallic constituents of the same clearly identifies it as high tin bronze. Chase's methodology explains the cause of rising of tin constituents to a higher value, due to dissolving of copper from the corrosion products. Silver content in these three specimens indicate the presence of it in copper ores.

Chattopadhyay observes that in manufacturing knobbed vessel, the present study revealed that initially it was cast in sand moulds and then it was hot worked after reheating in charcoal fired furnace. Then it was hammered into a vessel by alternate heating and forging. The finishing process perhaps comprized hammering with wooden mallet and subsequently heating and quenching was carried out. The non-existence of dendrites as well as the absence of twins on one hand and internal structure of martensite showing random dislocations and stacking faults on the other, clearly indicates the quenching process (Singh & Chattopadhyay, 2002 : 101-106).

4

Seals and Sealings

A seal is an engraved stamp bearing, singly or collectively a device, mark or letters pertaining to its owner. A sealing is an impression of such a stamp on a substance such as clay, wax, etc., and capable of being attached to a document to authenticate it or serve as signature or cognizance. An impression on a lump of clay placed over the knot of a cord binding a parcel protects its contents from being tampered with. Such sealings of baked clay bearing string mark on the back have been found in excavations at several sites.

Seals and sealings have a great historical value as one of the most reliable sources of early Indian history. While inscriptions tend to exaggerate and present facts with embellishments, the legends on seals and sealings are brief, compact and matter of fact. Hence they can be fully relied upon.

Seals throw valuable light on the past, revealing in particular the political and administrative situation and the socio-religious conditions of contemporary society. Keeping in view the above-noted value of seals, we present below a description as well as the historical significance of the seven seals and sealings obtained from Agiabir excavations.

The seal recorded from Agiabir belongs to a special category. It was recovered from inside a room near the suspected main entrance on the eastern side of Mound 2. It bears five letters engraved in Brahmi characters of early fourth century AD having legend 'Skandanaga'. Another sealing bearing the legend 'Harisenasya' in pre-Gupta Brahmi characters was recovered from trench YE-6-II. The small head marks on *ra*, extended upper portion of letter *sha* on either side and the angular form of *sa* in letter *sya* indicate that the palaeography of this sealing belongs to the late third or early fourth century AD. The other sealing having legend 'Rudrapalasya' in Gupta Brahmi characters was discovered from trench YE 6-I at the main mound. These two sealings bear symbols only.

A special category of seal impression was used in ancient times as a passport which enabled the courier entrance to or exit from a particular place.

The stratigraphic details of the seal and sealing is given in the following Table 4.1 :

TABLE 4.1

Sl. No.	*Accession No.*	*Year*	*Trench*	*Locus*	*Depth*	*Stratum*
1.	596A	1998-99 NW 1.22 m	YE 16/III	NE 1.35 x	1.05 m	(2)
2.	913A	1999-2000	YE 6-II	SE 1.50 m x NE 2.15 m	4.50 m	Unstratified
3.	1119	2000-01	YE6-I	SW 2.00 m x NW3.50 m	1.25-1.30 m	Pit 1SB(2)
4.	1146	2000-01	YE 6-IV	SE 3.00 m x SW 2.40 m	2.25-2.30 m	(4)
5.	1254	2000-01	YE 6-III-IV	NE 1.02 m x	5.65-5.70 m	(10)
6.	1137	2000-01	YE 6-IV	SE 2.00 m x	1.70 m	Pit 1 SB (2)
7.	1147	2000-01	YE 6-III	—	2.50 m	(4)

A detailed description of these antiquities is given below :

(Pl. XXI-A) A complete seal of ivory having light yellowish colour. The legend comprises five letters in the Brahmi characters of early fourth century AD which reads 'Skandnaga'. On the reverse a hole was made at the conical side.

Size : 3.48 cm x 2.86 cm; shape-conical

ABR /1999, Trench YE 16/III, Depth 1.05 m, Stratum (2)

(Pl. XXI-B) A complete sealing of baked clay having smoky grey colour. It bears a bow and arrow in the upper register while there is an inscription in early Gupta Brahmi characters which reads 'Harisenasya'.

Size-2.86 cm x 2.75 cm; Shape-Oval

ABR/ 2000, Trench YE 6/II, Depth 4.50m, Stratum-Unstratified

(Pl. XXII-A, No. 1.) An oval sealing of baked clay, smoky grey in colour. It depicts a standing horse in the lower register. The legend inscribed in Gupta Brahmi characters reads 'Rudrapalasya'. On the reverse, which is concave, string marks are visible.
Size-2.81 cm x 2.65 cm; Shape-Oval

ABR/ 2001, Trench YE 6/I, Depth 1.25-1.30 m, Stratum-Pit 1 SB (2).

No. 2. Sealing of baked clay, smoky grey in colour. It bears three letters which are indistinct. The reverse bears prominent string marks.

Size-2.37 cm x 2.08 cm; Shape-Oval

ABR/ 2001, Trench YE 6/IV, Depth, 2.25-2.30 m, Stratum-(4).

No. 3. A complete sealing of baked clay having smoky grey colour. It bears the symbol 

Size-2.65 cm x 2.30 cm; Shape-Oval

ABR/ 2001, Trench YE 5/ IV, Depth, 1.70 m, Stratum-Pit 1 SB(2).

No. 4. A broken sealing of baked clay, smoky grey in colour. The marks are indistinct and cannot be deciphered.

Size-2.80 cm x 1.80 cm; Shape-Oval

ABR/ 2001, Trench YE 6/ III-IV, Depth, 5.65-5.70 m, Stratum-(10).

No. 5. Sealing of smoky grey colour, oval in shape. It bears the symbol ▲. On the reverse it has very clear string marks.
Size-2.50 cm x 2.17 cm; Shape-Oval

ABR/ 2001, Trench YE 5/ III, Depth, 2.50 m, Stratum-(4).

As will be seen from the description given above, there are one seal and two sealings which bear the legends 'Skandanaga' and 'Harisenasya' respectively. All the three seals belong to Period IV dated to the first three centuries of the Christian era. The palaeography denotes that they can be securely dated to the early Gupta period. As regards their use, it is very clear that they had been used for sending the merchandise for trade. It may be noted that Agiabir is located on the banks of the Ganga, almost half way between Allahabad and Varanasi. There were several early historical cities like Rajghat (ancient Varanasi)on the one hand and Jhusi, Bhita, Kausambi and Sringaverapura on the other and the discovery of these seals and sealings proves that the traders of Agiabir were taking an active part in this riverine trade. Particular mention may be made of the sealing bearing the legend 'Harisenasya'. More than 400 sealings of this trader were unearthed in the excavations at Rajghat and the motifs depicted on them are exactly the same as the present one (Narain & Roy, 1977 : 14). This further testifies to the close relationship Agiabir had with ancient Varanasi (Rajghat).

The ivory seal with the legend 'Skandanaga' has a depiction of a peacock on it. We are told that peacock had also been depicted on the seals obtained from Bhita. A comparative study of the seals obtained from Bhita and Agiabir will provide further interesting links between the two sites. We know that the peacock is associated with the cult of *Karttikeya* as the latter's *vahana.* A seal from Bhita bearing the legend 'Sriskandsurasya' has a peacock standing to the left with the tail fanned out (Thaplyal, 1972 : 127). In this case the *vahana* was appropriately chosen as a seal device. The seal in the present collection also bears the name *'Skanda'* and the association of *'Skanda'* with his *vahana* peacock is very obvious.

Other sealings of this collection which do not bear the name of any individual or string mark on their backs were presumably used as tokens, passports or identity cards (marks of official authentication) or as votive offerings.

The sealing bearing the legend 'Rudrapalasya' has the depiction of a horse on it. A sealing from Rajghat has a winged horse shown on it (Thaplyal, 1972 : 275, fig. 31 No. 12). Horse has been depicted on the *Ashwamedha* type of coins of Samudragupta and other rulers of the Gupta dynasty.

5

Other Finds

THE LITHIC INDUSTRY

The lithic component which has been excavated from Period I at Agiabir comprises among the excavated materials a sizeable collection of chips, flakes, bladelets, cores and retouchers, etc.

The Agiabir lithic industry includes chips, flakes, bladelets, cores, retoucher and microlith (Fig. 22). Besides, some nodules of stones were also found. This group is significant as it suggests local chiselling of stone and import of raw material at the site. The stone lumps used here were banded agate, chert, jasper, quartz and chalcedony.

The representative types have been described below:

FIG. 22

1. Bladelet made on quartz. It has been utilized. Trench A-1 depth 195-200 cm. Layer (4).
2. Bladelet made on quartz. It has been retouched. Trench A-1, depth 183-190 cm. Layer (4).
3. Prepared core made on banded agate. Core with prepared dorsal surface and unprepared striking platform. Trench A-1, depth 185-190 cm. Layer (4).
4. Bladelet made on banded agate. It has been utiled. Trench A-1; depth 195-200 cm. Layer (4).
5. Long dressing chip of banded agate. Trench A-1; depth 185-190 cm. Layer (4).
6. Bladelet made on banded agate. It has a faceted striking platform. Trench A-1; depth 185-190 cm. Layer (4).

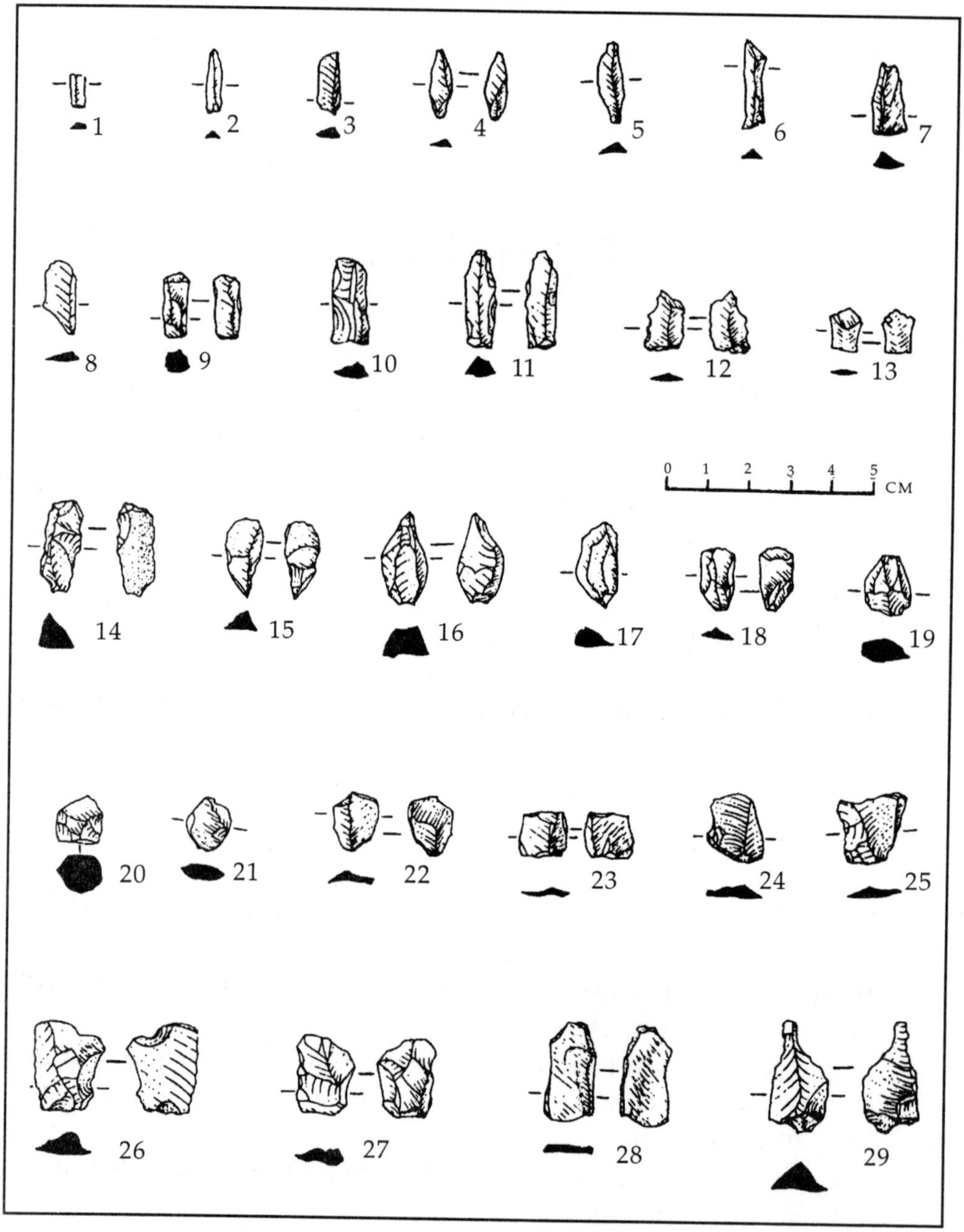

Fig. 22. Microliths of Agiabir, Period I.
Bladelets, cores and dressing chips of quartz and agate, Period I.

7. Dressing chip of banded agate. Trench A-1; depth 195-200 cm. Layer (4).
8. Dressing chip of banded agate. Trench. A-1; depth 185-190 cm. Layer (4).
9. Prepared core made on banded agate. Core with unprepared dorsal surface and prepared striking platform. Trench A-1; depth 185-190 cm. Layer (4).
10. Bladelet made on banded agate. It has an unfaceted striking platform. Trench A-1; depth 185-190 cm. Layer (4).
11. Thick long prepared core. Core with prepared dorsal surface and prepared striking platform. Trench A-1; depth 195-200 cm. Layer (4).
12. Small dressing chip of banded agate. Trench A-1; depth 180-185 cm. Layer (4).
13. Small dressing chip of banded agate. Trench A-1; depth 180-185 cm. Layer (4).
14. Bladelet made on jasper. It has a prepared ridge in the centre. Trench A-1; depth 185-200 cm. Layer (4).
15. Triangular dressing chip of banded agate. Trench A-1; depth 185-190 cm. Layer (4).
16. Flattened core made on banded agate. From the dorsal surface a few micro blades have been detached. Under-surface retains dressed striking platform and a good portion of cortex. Trench A-1; depth 185-190 cm. Layer (4).
17. Dressing chip of banded agate. Trench A-1; depth 185-190 cm. Layer (4).
18. Small dressing chip of banded agate. Trench A-1; depth 185-190 cm. Layer (4).
19. Small dressing chip of banded agate. Trench A-1; depth 185-190 cm. Layer (4).
20. Small undressing chip of banded agate. Trench A-1; depth 185-190 cm. Layer (4).
21. Unprepared core made on quartz. Trench A-1; depth 185-190 cm. Layer (4).
22. Dressing chip of banded agate. Trench A-1; depth 185-190 cm. Layer (4).
23. Small dressing chip of banded agate. Trench A-1; depth 185-190 cm. Layer (4).

24. Dressing chip of banded agate. Trench A-1; depth 185-190 cm. Layer (4).
25. Dressing chip of banded agate. Trench A-1; depth 185-190 cm. Layer (4).
26. This flake of chert retains core preparation marks and a part of cortex. Trench A-1; depth 185-190 cm. Layer (4).
27. Dressing chip of banded agate. Trench A-1; depth 185-190 cm. Layer (4).
28. Long dressing chip of banded agate. Trench A-1; depth 185-190 cm. Layer (4).
29. Triangular unprepared flake made on banded agate. Trench A-1; depth 185-190 cm. Layer (4).

The lithic collection brings out the fact the Agiabir was involved in lithic crafts for two purposes: (i) for the production of stone beads and (ii) for the production of microliths. It is interesting to note that for both the categories of artefacts similar group of stones were used. All the types of stones used by earliest settlers of Agiabir were imported at the site, since the thick alluvial cover around the site is completely devoid of lithic resources. As has been postulated for other prehistoric settlements of inland alluvial plains of Uttar Pradesh (Sharma *et al.*, 1980), it may be held that the stones utilized at Agiabir were also brought by the migrating groups from the Vindhyas. The most common stones used at this site were agate (91.30 per cent); quartz (4.35 per cent), jasper (1.09 per cent) and chert (3.26 per cent). Agate was preferred most among the three as it was the hardest stone. It may be the reason for using this stone for making beads in good frequency.

BEADS (Pls. XXII-B, XXIII, XXIV)

In the Indian context, beads of various raw materials are the important constituent of the assemblage of the antiquities recovered from any excavation, at least from the Chalcolithic period onwards. Some of the important production centres belonging to the different cultural phases are Mohenjo-daro (Kenoyer, 1986; Tosi *et al.*, 1984), Chanhu-Daro (Mackay, 1943), Lothal (Rao, 1973), Arikamedu (Wheeler *et al.*, 1946), Ujjain (Banerjee, 1959) and Kodumanal (Rajan, 1990).

The excavation yielded 101 beads of stone, 311 beads of faience, besides beads of bone, shell and ivory; together with 169 beads of terracotta raising the total number to 590. They are variously distributed in the first three periods. Period I-43, Period II-46, Period III-413. Materialwise, this

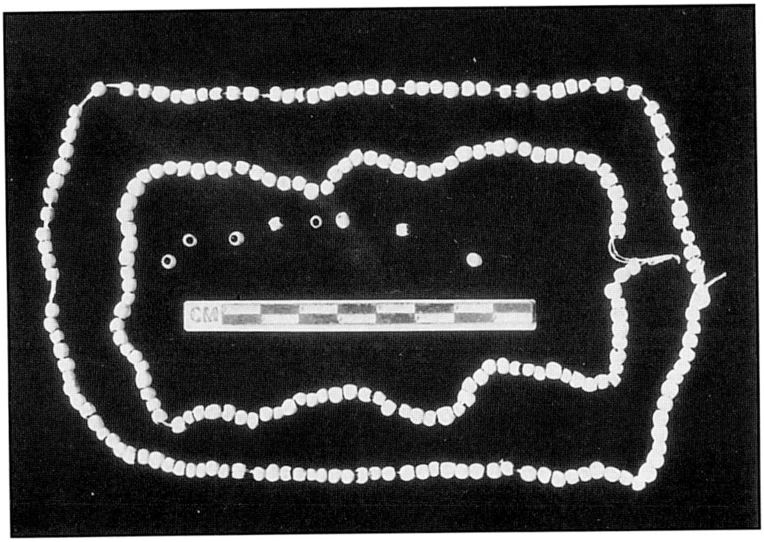

Pl. XXVA. Beads of faience, Period III.

Pl. XXVIA. Microphotograph of faience bead showing angular quartz, Period III. →

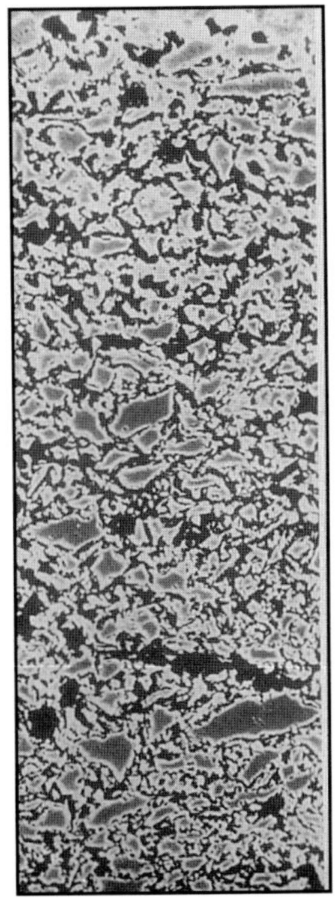

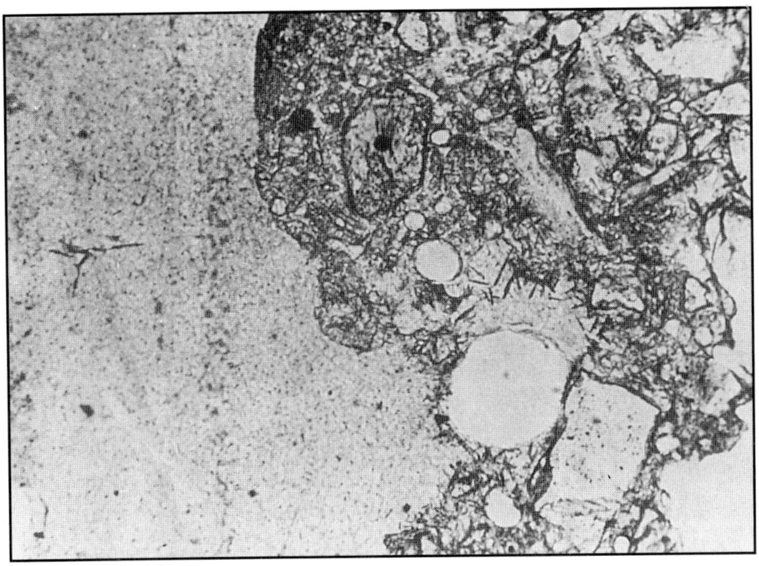

Pl. XXVB. Microphotograph of faience bead showing glassy phase, Period III.

Pl. XXVIB. Microphotograph of faience bead, liquid silicate, Period III. →

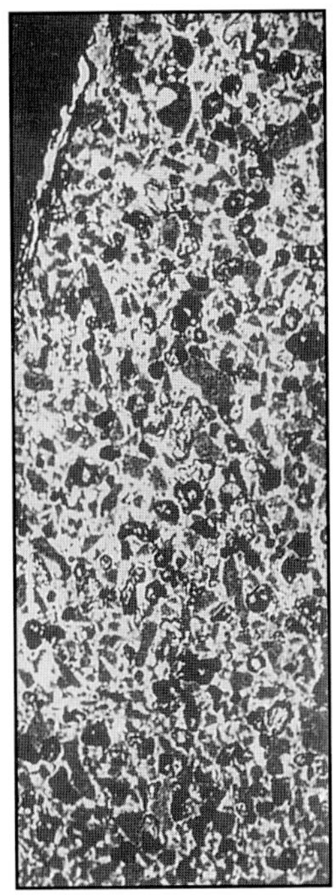

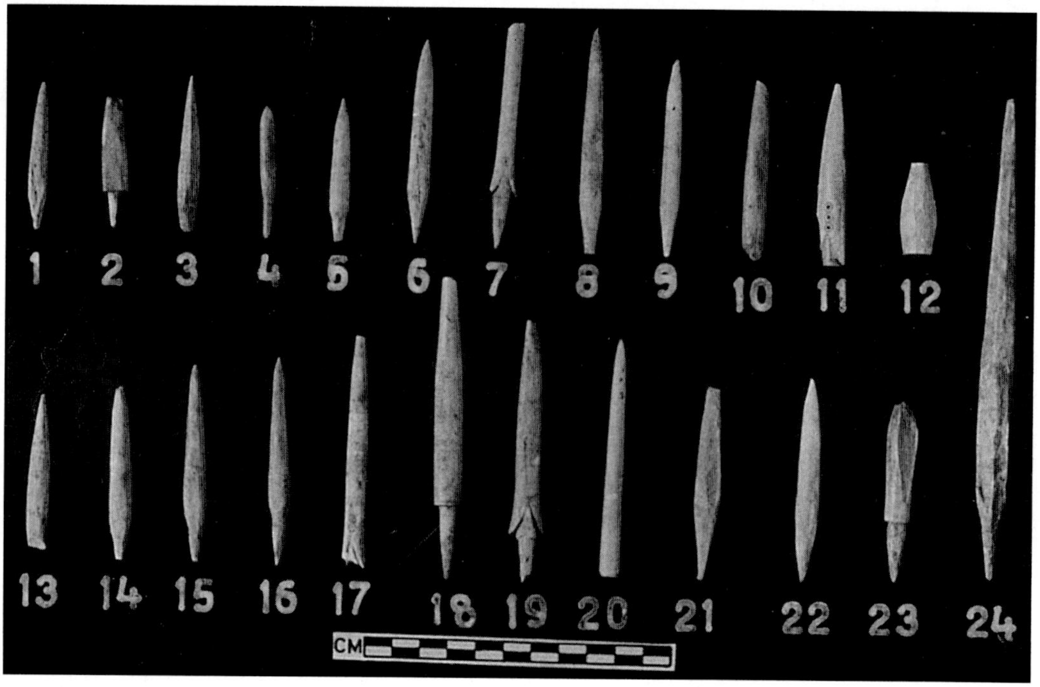

Pl. XXVIIA. Bone points and arrowheads, Periods I & II.

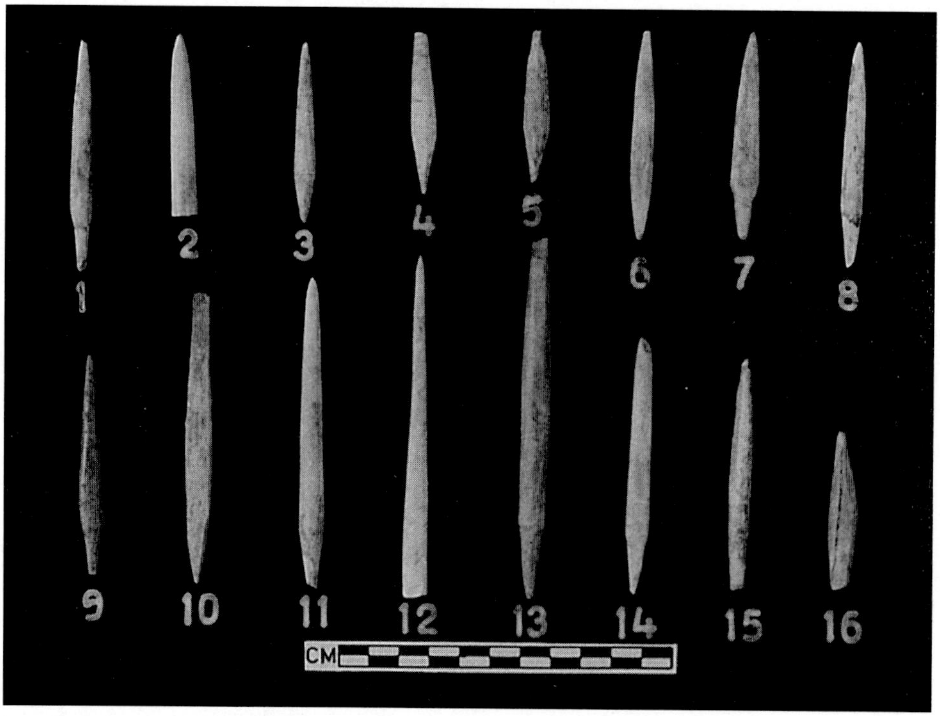

Pl. XXVIIB. Bone points, Periods III & IV.

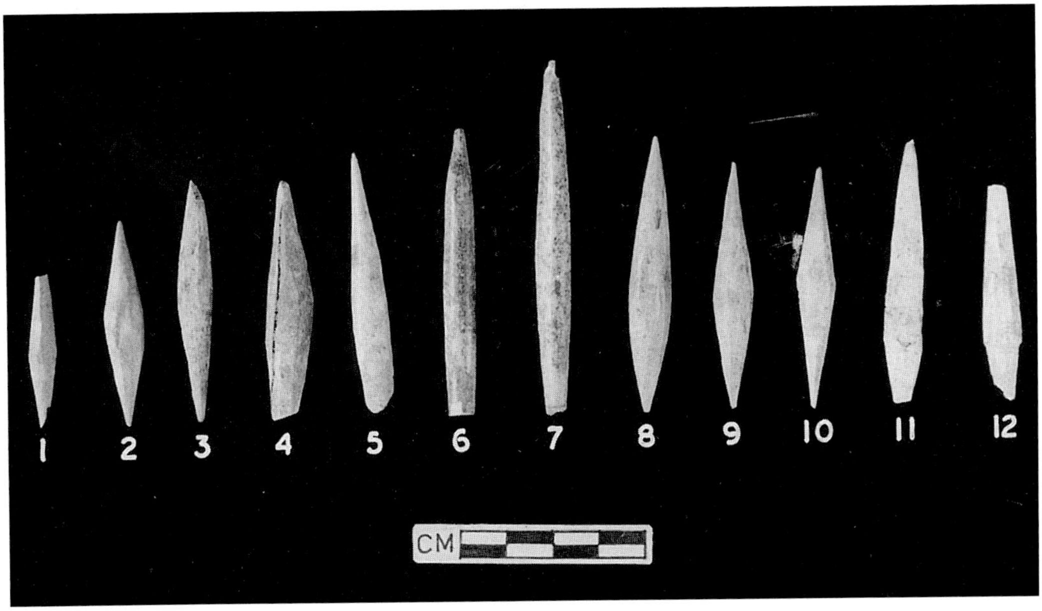

Pl. XXVIIIA. Bone points, Periods III & IV.

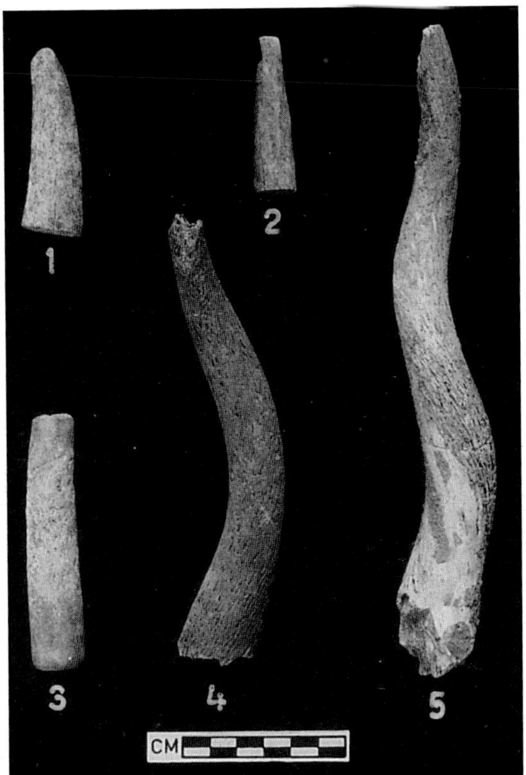

Pl. XXVIIIB. Antlers of Period II, III & IV.

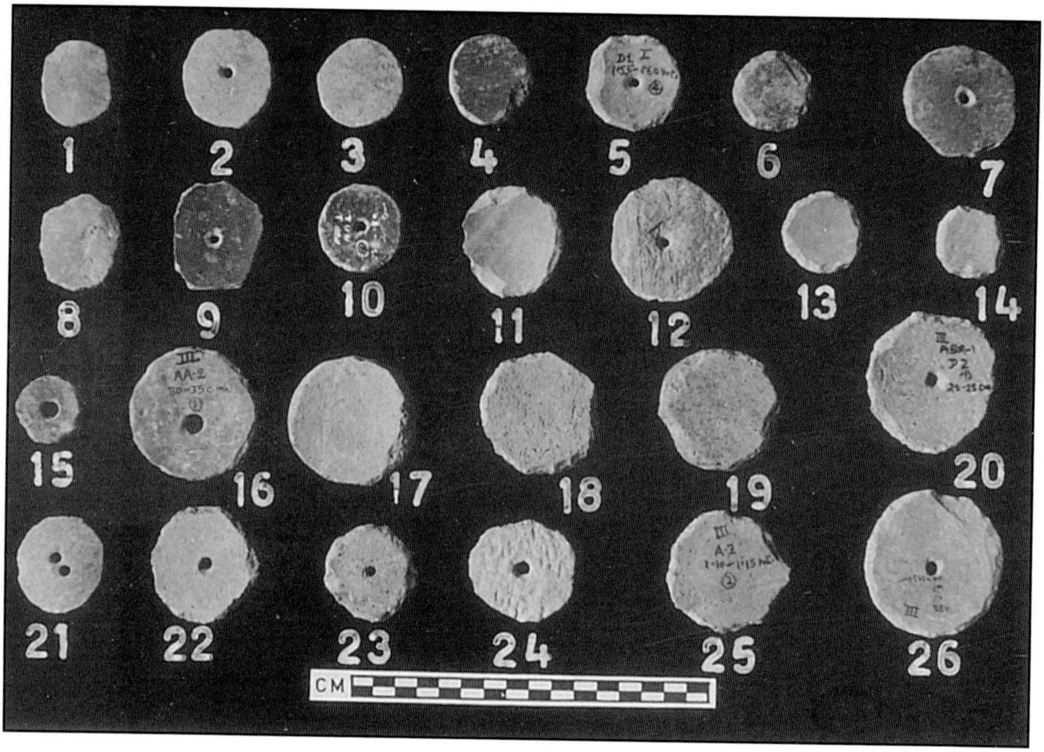

Pl. XXIXA. Pottery discs from Periods I, II & III.

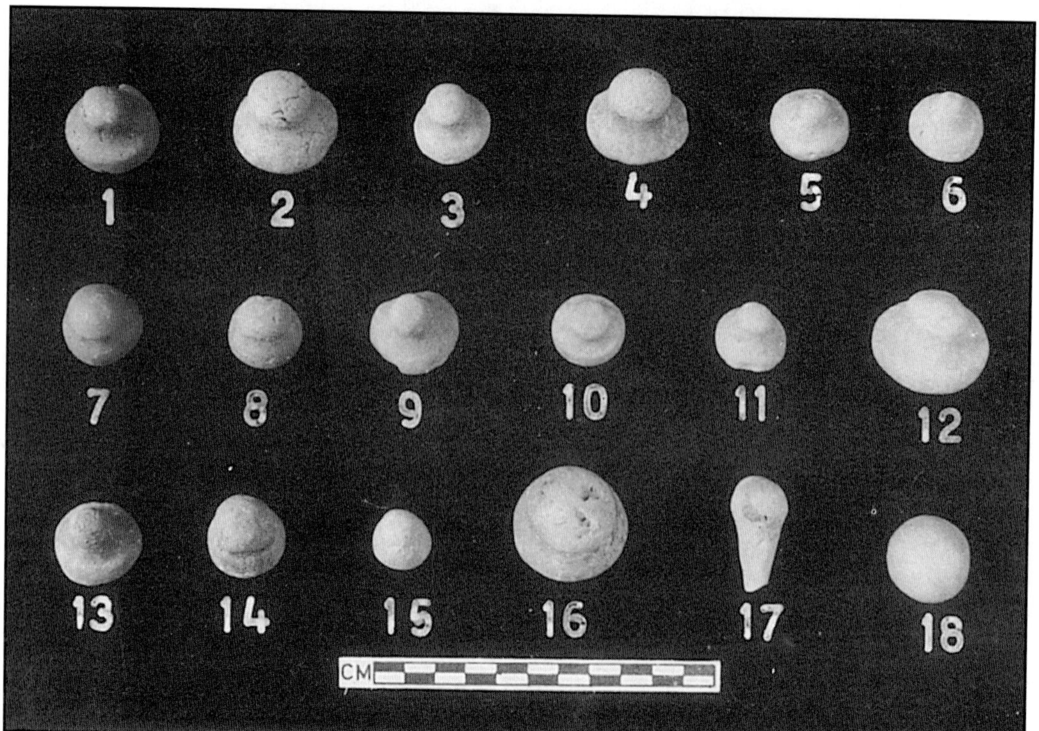

Pl. XXIXB. Gamesmen from Periods I, II & III.

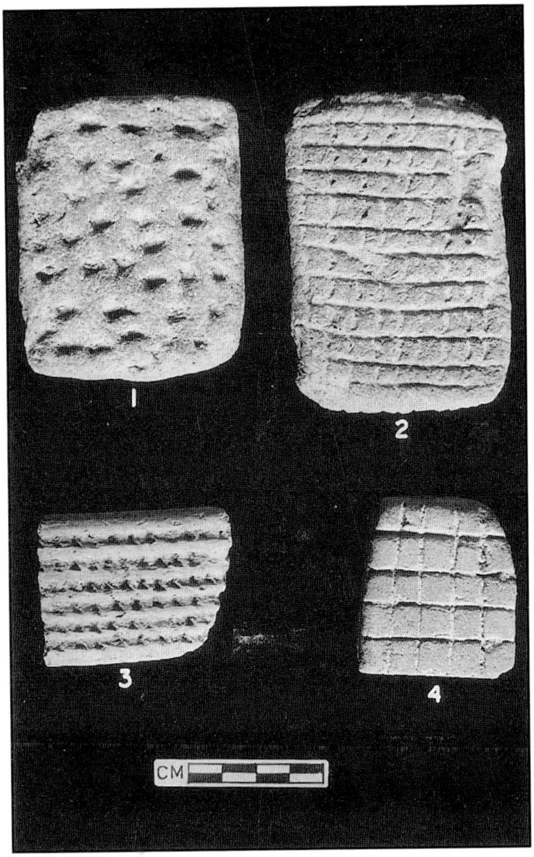

Pl. XXXA. Skin rubbers, Period III.

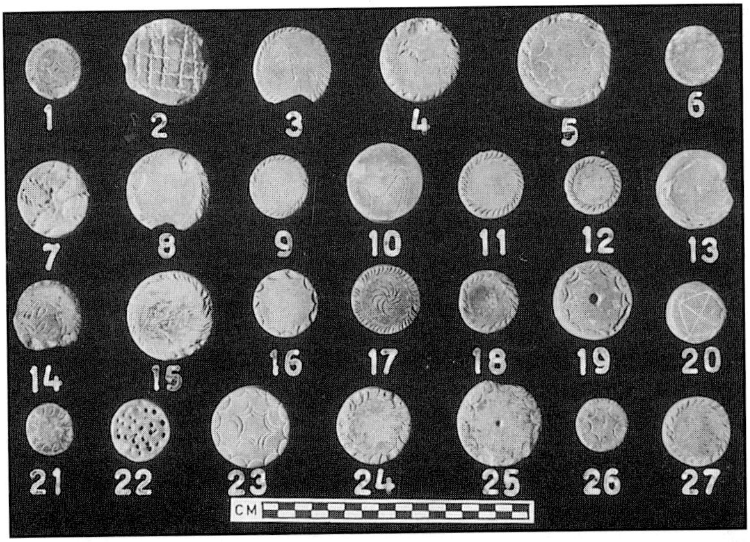

Pl. XXXB. Terracotta discs from Periods II & III.

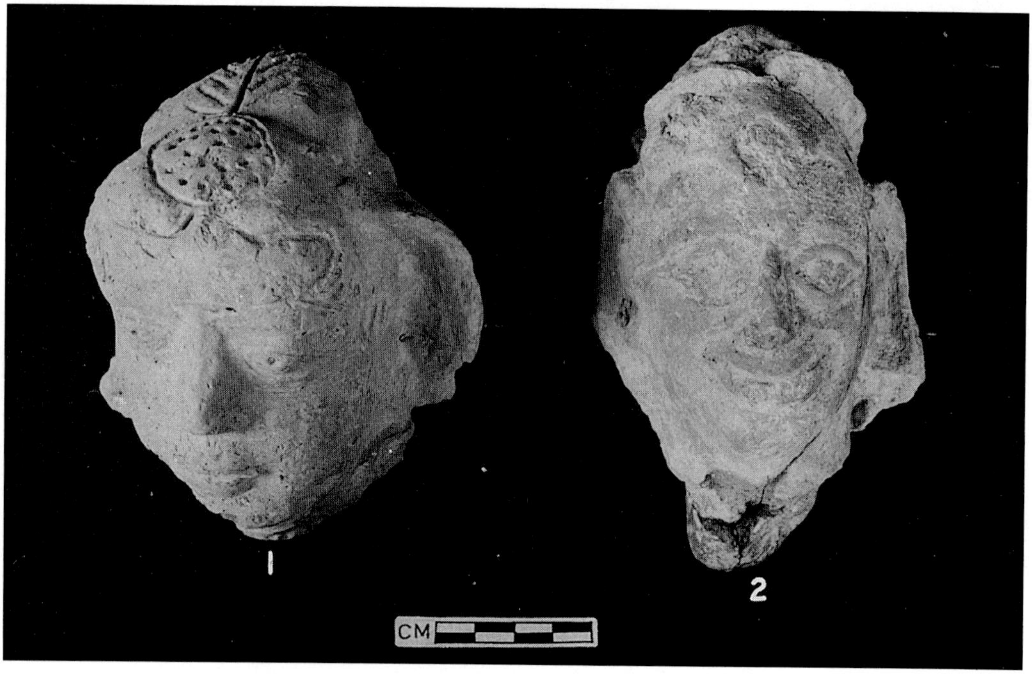

Pl. XXXIA. Terracotta human figurines, Period IV.

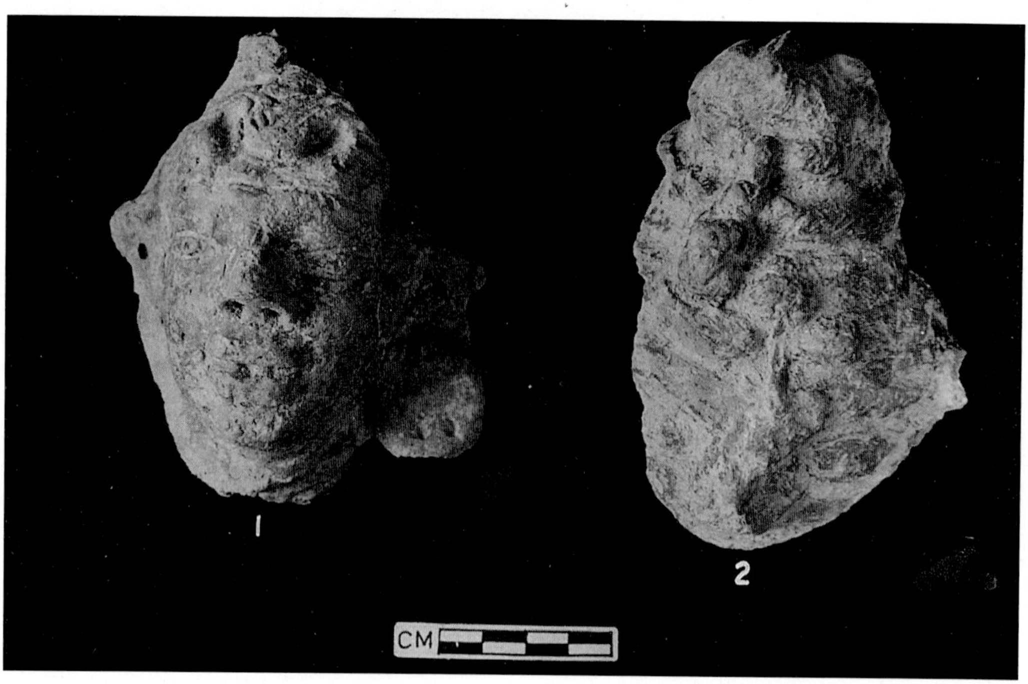

Pl. XXXIB. Terracotta human figurines, Period IV.

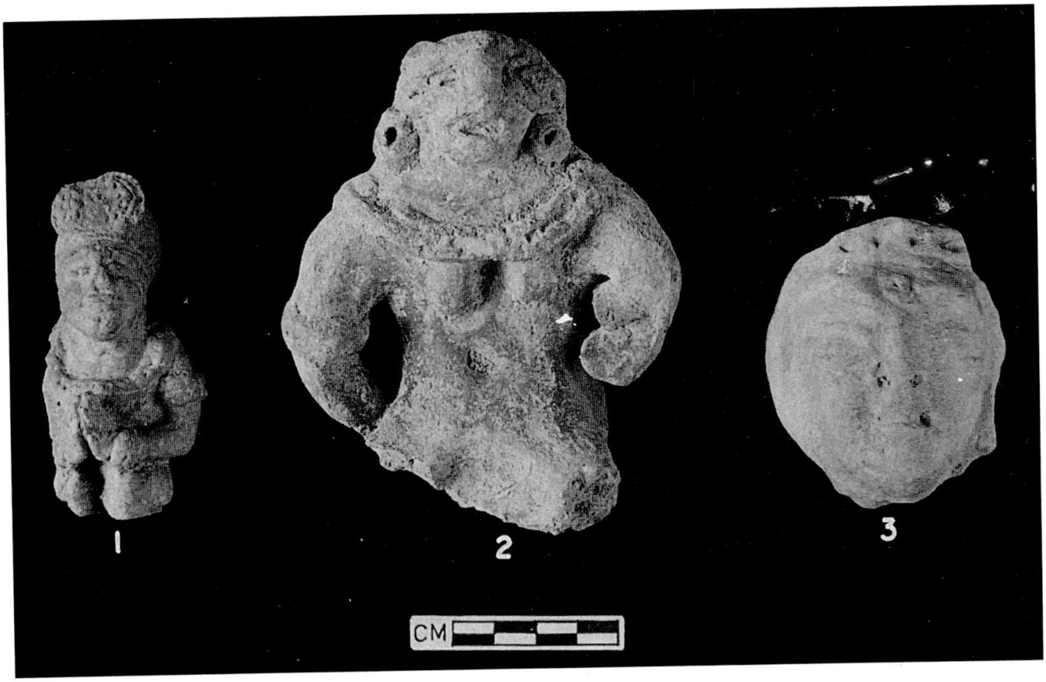

Pl. XXXIIA. Terracotta human figurines, Period IV.

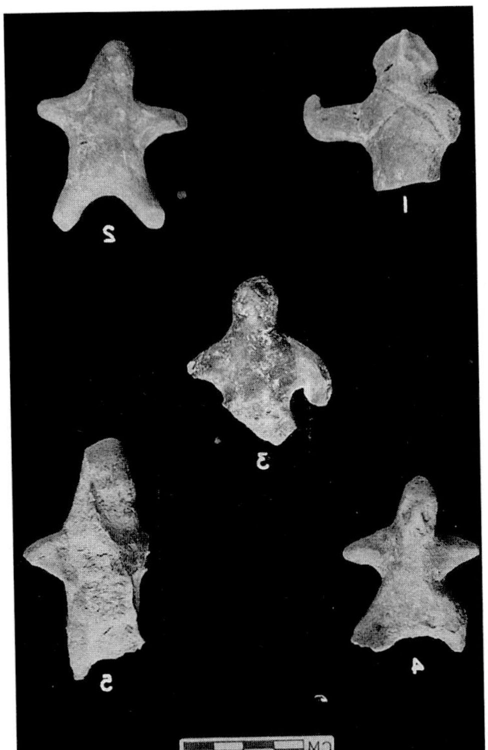

Pl. XXXIIB. Star-shaped figurines, Periods IV & V.

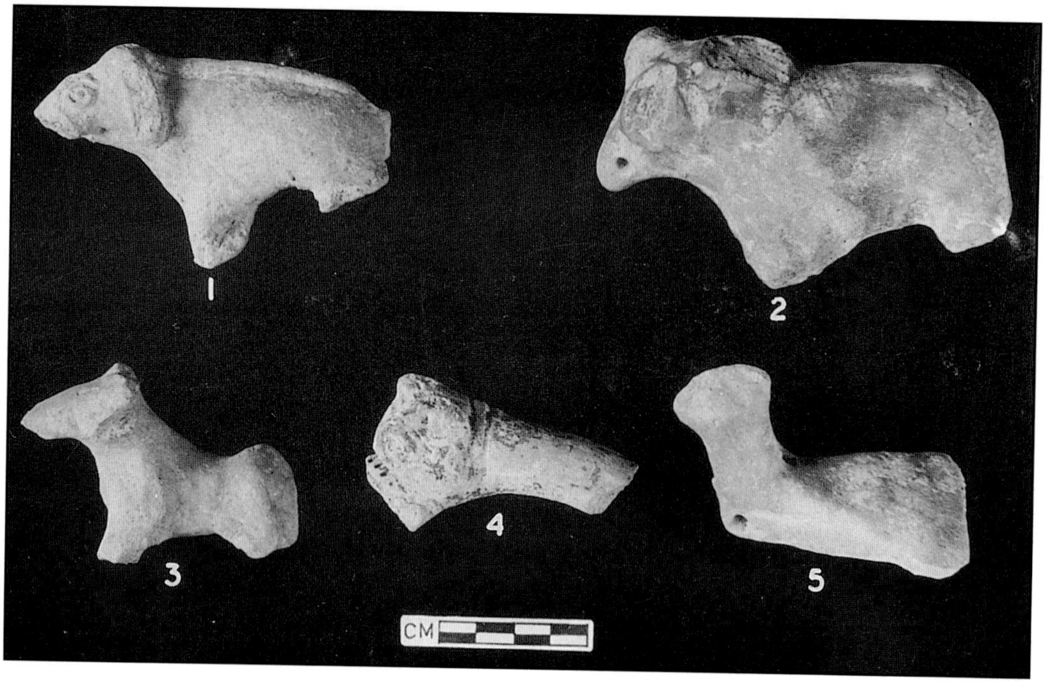

Pl. XXXIIIA. Terracotta animal figurines, Periods IV & V.

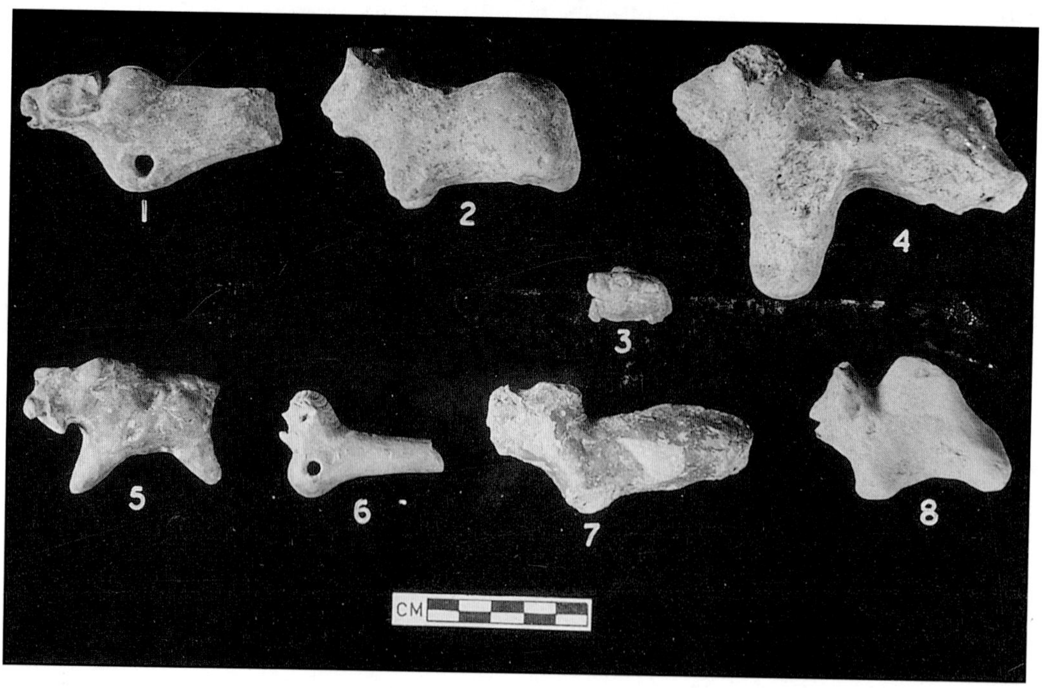

Pl. XXXIIIB. Terracotta animal figurines, Period V.

collection is not very impressive as among the semi-precious stones, agate and carnelian are the only important materials represented by 56 and 20 beads respectively. Chert, jasper, quartz and glass are the other three materials represented by 4, 2, 4 and 15 beads respectively. Among other materials mention may be made of faience, bone, shell and ivory but the number of beads in all these materials except faience is very meagre. Among the stone beads agate is the only material whose beads were produced locally. This tradition of bead making started from the first habitation at the site and it continued in the subsequent two periods. This statement is substantiated by the fact that 8, 5 and 8 unfinished beads of agate were found from the first three periods of this site. The periodwise distribution of beads found in the excavations is as Table 5.1:

TABLE 5.1

Types	*I*	*II*	*III*	*IV*	*V*	*Total*
Agate	19 (8 Unfinished)	11 (5 Unfinished)	19 (8 Unfinished)	06	01	56
Bone	01	-	-	-	01	02
Carnelian	02	01	15	02	-	20
Chert	-	-	02	01	01	04
Faience	03	03	305*	-	-	311
Glass	-	02	04	07	02	15
Ivory	-	-	03	-	-	03
Jasper	-	-	01	01	-	02
Quartz	-	-	01	01	02	04
Shell	01	01	01	-	01	04
Terracotta						
i)*Ghata*-shaped	05	18	40	12	13	88
ii) Arecanut	12	10	22	20	17	81
Total	**43**	**46**	**413**	**50**	**38**	**590**

* A hoard of about 300 faience beads was recovered from Period III.

Among the terracotta beads, the most popular types are *ghata*-shaped and arecanut shaped. These shapes are represented by 88 and 81 specimens respectively (Pl. XXIV-B). Similar beads have been recovered from Rajghat and other sites. Some *ghata*-shaped beads having larger opening have been described as net shinkers by some scholars (Francis, 1978-79 : 95-99). Seventeen such examples were found from this excavation and all are confined to Period I only.

A hoard of about 300 faience beads (Pl. XXV-A) placed in a miniature vessel of black slipped ware is the other noteworthy find. Ten beads from this hoard were subjected to the scientific examinations (Singh & Singh, 2000 : 65-68) and the following account is based on their study. In addition, a few samples were prepared for petrological studies from the broken pieces in order to characterize them by ascertaining their mineral as well as chemical compositions. The descriptions of beads along with their weights, colour, hardness and the specific gravities are given in the Table 5.2.

TABLE 5.2

Sl.	*Arch. No.*	*Period*	*Colour*	*Weight (gm.)*	*Hardness*	*Sp. Gravity*
1.	ABR 338	I	Blue-Green	0.025	4-5	2.41
2.	ABR 281	I	Light-Blue	0.0149	4	2.39
3.	ABR 90	II	Light-Blue	0.0276	5	2.49
4.	ABR 388	III	Light-Blue	0.0834	5	2.48
5.	ABR 388 / 1	III	Light-Blue	0.0249	5	2.50
6.	ABR 388 / 2	III	Light-Blue	0.0199	4-5	2.51
7.	ABR 388 / 3	III	Light-Blue	0.0151	5	2.49
8.	ABR 388 / 4	III	Light-Blue	0.0206	5	2.48
9.	ABR 388 / 5	III	Light-Blue	0.0356	5	2.47
10.	ABR 388 /6	III	Light-Blue	0.026	4-5	2.49

In the history of ceramics, faience is almost the first 'contrived' non-clay body developed as a white ground for the use of blue-green colour in the imitation of lapis lazuli and turquoise (Kingery & Vandiver, 1986 : 51-56).

Like most ancient faience it consists of a quite porous and weak body coated with a glassy glaze. Chemical analyses were done with wet-chemical method to ascertain oxides compositions as given in the Table 5.3.

TABLE 5.3. CHEMICAL COMPOSITION OF FAIENCE BEADS

Constituents	*Agiabir*		*Rajghat*	
	ABR-338	*ABR-368*	*RGT-399*	*RGT-803*
SiO_2	87.97	87.14	86.87	84.86
$Fe_2\ O_3$	0.80	1.81	1.21	0.97
Al_2O_3	3.16	4.01	3.96	4.71
CaO	0.27	1.25	0.87	1.81
MgO	0.69	-	0.37	0.87
Na_2O	3.82	4.50	-	-
K_2O	0.76	0.66	-	-
CuO	0.47	0.80	0.49	0.91
MnO	-	trace	-	trace
TIO_2	0.01	-	-	-
PO_4	0.70	-	-	-

It is evident that the powdered samples show granular structure and when examined under a low power microscope it was confirmed as quartz. The percentage of silica is lesser than that at Harappa but similar to Rajghat, i.e. 87.97 and 87.14. We see that the body has very little residual alkali but retained the insoluble lime and iron impurities. The blue-green tints of the beads are due to the oxides of copper. Dissolved in the glaze, the iron oxide impurity contributes a greenish colour, but is inconsequential in comparison to the copper oxide. High alumina (3.16 and 4.01) has checked the devitrification of the beads. The intermediate white quartz layer contains more alkali and copper showing that the slurry used was made up with more of these constituents to form the efflorescent glaze. The soda contents of the glaze increases. The firing temperature for such glaze must have been in the range of 800-900° C.

The microstructures of the body, fine white powdered quartz and glaze as given in the above table illustrate how a small fraction of liquid silicate formed at the high temperature, bonds the quartz particles together. They consist of a fragmented core of angular quartz with varying amount of interstitial glass.

From these observations, Singh and Singh concluded that the bonding of quartz particles of the body mass, brought about by the firing process, consists essentially of the formation of a relatively small amount of crypto crystalline along the grain boundaries, without the production of a significant amount of glassy phase. Brown colour iron oxide is seen in fine grain as a cementing material.

Although, so far no furnace or oven and raw materials associated with the use of the manufacturing of faience beads have been identified in the limited excavation but on the basis of the results of the preliminary study and the experiments conducted on ancient faience by Tite *et al.* (1983 : 17-27) and Wulff (1968 : 98-107), it can be suggested that, the faience beads of Agiabir were made of modelling or moulding a mixture of fine quartz or sand and small amount of lime and alkali with copper salts that furnished the blue-green colour. A mixture of such raw materials with water is stiff at first, but becomes soft and flowing when it is deformed, if deformed too rapidly, it cracks. During drawing, the soluble salts migrate to the surface and a layer of effloresced salts is deposited as the water evaporates. Upon firing, these salts react with the quartz body to form the glaze layer. When drying is more rapid, more salts are deposited and so glaze is thicker. In the inner portion where drying is slower, the glaze is thinner. Salt-glazing by the firing of effloresced salts at temperature of 800-900° C has been the prime method of manufacture of faience objects in other parts of the world during second-third millennium BC (Tite *et al.*, 1983 :17-27) which is noticed at Agiabir also.

BONE POINTS (Pls. XXVII & XXVIII)

The excavation yielded as many as 205 objects of bone and ivory which are described as points and arrowheads in archaeological parlance. Their periodwise distribution at the present site is as in Table 5.4:

TABLE 5.4

Types	*I*	*II*	*III*	*IV*	*V*	*Total*
A. Points	09	28	47	12	05	101
B. Arrowheads						
i) Tanged	-	23	58	11	02	94
ii) Socketed	-	02	03	-	-	05
iii) Barbed & socketed	-	01	-	-	-	01
iv) Barbed & Tanged	-	04	-	-	-	04
Total	**09**	**58**	**108**	**23**	**07**	**205**

The distribution of these antiquities largely tallies with this class of antiquities from Narhan. Although these antiquities are present in all the five periods, they predominate in Period II and III. Their number decreases in the subsequent two periods presumably because these stratas are highly disturbed and robbed. As has been stated elsewhere (Singh, 1994 : 176), arrowheads are mainly concentrated in 800-200 BC levels in the Ganga Plain. The bone points and arrowheads obtained from Agiabir perfectly fit into this time frame. Tanged and barbed arrowheads are present at Agiabir also but those with punch circlet designs engraved on them are comparatively limited in number. Such designs have been noticed on three of them (Pl. XXVII-A, Nos. 7, 11 and 19). Similar objects have been reported from the PGW levels as well as NBPW levels at Atranjikhera (Gaur, 1983, Fig. 63, No. 4, Fig. 118, No. 1). Some specimens are unusually large and one tanged arrowhead measures 24 cm. (Pl. XXVII-A, No. 24).

HOPSCOTCHES (Pl. XXIX-A)

The hopscotches of various periods vary in size. Among those of Period I, the smallest ones measure 2.5 cm in diameter while the largest ones measure 7.5 cm. Their average size is roughly about 4.6 cm. In Period III also, their size remains more or less the same. The smallest hopscotches of Period II measure 2.5 cm while the largest have a diameter of 9 cm. Their average size is about 5 cm. In Period III also their average size remains the same; the smallest having a diameter of 2.5 cm and the largest about 5 cm. Their periodwise distribution is as in Table 5.5 :

TABLE 5.5

Types	*I*	*II*	*III*	*IV*	*V*	*Total*
1. Unperforated	53	141	178	17	08	397
2. Perforated (with single perforation)	10	14	16	02	03	45
3. Perforated (with double perforation)	-	-	01	-	-	01
Total	**63**	**155**	**195**	**19**	**11**	**443**

A class of antiquities variously described as pottery discs, hopscotches or gaming counters have been documented from various sites in the Ganga Plain, mostly from the PGW and the NBPW levels. Such antiquities have also been reported from Narhan culture in the Sarayupar plain. As given in the above table, no less than 443 specimens of this type have been reported from the limited excavations at Agiabir, demonstrating their popularity as well as prolific use. Sixty three antiquities of this type have been reported from the earliest period but their number rises progressively to 155 in Period II and 195 in Period III. By far the commonest type of pottery disc are the unperforated ones which account for as many as 397 pieces. Among the remaining 46 pieces, 45 have single perforation and one has double perforations. All these pottery discs are invariably made of broken potsherds by cutting and grinding and giving them round, flat shapes.

GAMESMEN (Pl. XXIX-B)

A class of antiquities made of terracotta are known as gamesmen. The present excavation yielded 35 specimens. It continued to occur in Periods I, II and III. They are distributed as follows :

Period I—4, II—05, III—26.

SKIN RUBBERS (Pl. XXX-A)

The excavation yielded only four skin rubbers. They are all confined to Period III and are illustrated in Pl. XXX-A.

1. Rectangular skin rubber of terracotta with incised design on both the sides and of red colour with a wash. From Period III.
2. Rectangular skin rubber of terracotta with incised square design on both sides. The other side is comparatively smooth. From Period III.
3. A fragmentary rectangular shaped skin rubber of terracotta with deeply incised triangular notches between longitudinal grooves. From Period III.
4. Almost square skin rubber of terracotta with incised square design on both the sides and of red colour with a wash. From Period III.

TERRACOTTA DISCS (Pl. XXX-B)

In the limited excavations, as many as 244 terracotta discs were recovered. This is an unusually large number. They are unevenly distributed in Periods II, III and IV. Of these, as many as 62 came from Period II and 182 specimens were recovered from Period III. No terracotta disc was recovered from Period I. These discs are made of well-levigated clay and fired under oxidized condition, giving them a bright red surface colour. The designs are confined to the edges on both sides. The important designs are rope pattern and nail pattern. On some discs, an antelope like animal is carved (Pl. XXX B, Nos. 3, 10 & 15). Similar designs have been carved in some of the discs of Rajghat and Prahladpur.

TERRACOTTA FIGURINES (Pls. XXXI-XXXIII)

The excavation yielded 18 human and 15 animal figurines, some of them complete but most of them in broken condition. The selected specimens are given below :

Pl. XXXI-A

1. The large moulded head of a male figure, smiling face, well baked to give a red colour having bright red slip. From Period IV.
2. Moulded head of a male figure with elongated eyes, long aquiline nose and plump face. The ears are broken but there is a knot on the head with pressed design. It bears a bright red slip. The small tenon at the base of the neck suggests that the head was attached to the main body. From Period IV.

Pl. XXXI-B

1. A human head, partly broken, having an elongated face, thick lips and open mouth. This figure has long eyes presumably made by the same technique as in No. 2 above. From Period IV.
2. Broken human head with elongated eyes, badly damaged. From Period IV

Pl. XXXII-A

1. Male head, well-dressed hair. The hands are folded. From Period V.
2. Crudely modelled figure of *Naigmesa*, pronounced breasts, mouth with incised slit, dangling ears with small stretched hand. From Period IV.
3. Female head, headdress damaged, left ear broken off, well baked to give a red colour. From Period V.

Pl. XXXII-B

1. Crudely modelled mother goddess of smoky grey colour, pinched face, rising left arm. From Period III.
2. Crudely modelled figure of red colour and having bright red slip. From Period IV.
3. Crudely modelled figure of grey colour. From Period IV.
4. Crudely modelled figure, pinched face and hollow eye sockets. From Period V.

5. Broken figure of red colour and having bright red slip which is peeled off at places. From Period V.

Pl. XXXIII-A

1. Broken animal figurine of an elephant. From Period V.
2. *Ibid.*
3. Grotesque figure of a dog with bulky hind portion. From Period V.
4. Broken head portion of a lion. It has a bright red slip. From Period V.
5. Stylised figure of a bird. The body is coated with bright red slip. From Period V.

Pl. XXXIII-B

1. Figure of a bull. From Period IV.
2, Grotesque figure of a dog with bulky hind portion. From Period IV.
3. Figure of a dog. From Period IV.
4. Broken figure of a ram (?). This figure has bright red slip on the body and is badly damaged. From Period V.
5. Bull / *Nilgai* with comparatively heavy body; the horn, face and legs are broken. Fired to biscuit red colour. From Period III.
6. Small figure of unidentified animal. From Period IV.
7. Broken figure of an elephant. From Period IV.
8. Stylised figure of a bull. From Period V.

6

Epilogue

A careful analysis of the ceramic industries and other artefactual data from the limited excavations has brought forth the following facts :

1. As at other sites of Narhan culture excavated by us, Black-and-Red Ware was the principal ceramic industry of the first settlers of Agiabir. However, this ware has regional variations. It is marked by overall coarseness and fine fabric, a hallmark of the type-site of Narhan, is either completely absent or is present in limited number. Similarly, linear paintings in white, are very prolific at the type-site (where they account for 20 per cent) but are very limited at the present site.
2. While the *lota*-shaped vessel of Black-and-Red Ware has not been reported on sites of Sarayupar plain (Narhan, Imlidih Khurd and Dhuriapar), it is present at Agiabir as also at Waina in district Ballia (Singh *et al.*, 1996, Fig. 6, Nos. 2-5).
3. Some characteristic shapes like the *thali* are completely absent in the Black-and-Red Ware of Period I at Agiabir while this shape occurs at other sites of this region, namely-Raja-Nala-Ka-Tila and Malhar.
4. The inhabitants of Period I at Agiabir fully exploited the neighbouring Vindhyan hills. The easy accessibility of siliceous stones in the hills opposite this site led to the manufacture of beads and microliths locally. The presence of limited number of microliths at Agiabir and Waina is an important component. It may be noted that although beads were manufactured at Narhan, microliths are totally absent on all sites of the Sarayupar plains. It may be added that Agiabir was a bead manufacturing centre from the first period itself which continued for the subsequent two periods. As beads are an important item of trade, their manufacture and export added substantially to the prosperity of this township.

5. The presence of an unusually large number of terracotta discs and pottery discs documented in the limited excavations, demonstrates the richness of the cultures of subsequent two periods (Period II and III).
6. This fact is further substantiated by the occurrence of metal tools also. While Period I is almost totally devoid of metals (except a solitary fish-hook of copper), a large number of iron objects have been documented both from Period II and III. These comprise 30 tools and implements from Period II and 56 tools from Period III (NBPW period).
7. As has been noted above, no NBPW site in India has so far yielded metal vessels in such a large number. Iron lampstand of the mid phase of NBPW Period is a rare discovery. Such lampstands have not been found from any other site in India. The lamp of Taxila belongs to a later date. The prosperity and flourishing trade and economy of the NBPW culture of the Ganga Plain is well reflected by the recovery of this cache of metal objects. These findings are reflective of economic prosperity as also the contemporary social set up of this period.
8. The first settlers occupied the western part of Mound 1 and subsequent settlements gradually shifted to the eastern side along the Ganga. The maximum expansion of the township is seen during the mid phase of the NBPW period (*c.* 400 BC) when the population expanded to Mound-3 also. Some new types in NBPW like the handled dish indicates the prosperity of the site. There seems to be manifold increase in the prosperity of the site in Period IV (Sunga-Kushana Period). Well-built walls of burnt bricks have been exposed in the limited excavations conducted on the eastern fringe of the main mound (Pls. XV-XVI). This prosperity continued in the subsequent period and Agiabir played the part of an important trade centre as attested to by the discovery of an ivory seal bearing the legend *Skandanaga*. As Agiabir is situated between several township of considerable importance like Kausambi, Bhita and Jhusi on the west and Rajghat (ancient Varanasi) in the east with the mighty Ganga serving as the lifeline, it must have played a pivotal role in the brisk trade between these townships during the Early Historical period.
9. The limited excavation provides interesting details regarding the religious beliefs and rituals performed during the early centuries of the Christian era. That the cult of lotus headed goddess was prevalent in the Mid Ganga Valley in the early centuries of the Christian era, is proved by the discovery of terracotta figures of the goddess from Agiabir. Similar figures were reported earlier from Bhita, Kausambi

and Jhusi (Marshall, 1915 : 24-94). The cult of mother goddess with flat body, stumpy arms and legs, pendulous breasts and a cone like head has a hoary antiquity as mother goddess figures have been reported from Jorwe culture levels (*c.* 1300-1000 BC) at Inamgaon. The terracotta figures of this goddess obtained from Bhita, Kausambi and Jhusi are entirely nude and have a few ornaments including a girdle, armlets, necklace and anklets. These figures are identical to that found from Agiabir. They seem to represent a fertility female in the birth giving pose. They are taken to represent the Mother Earth, 'origin-ground' or birthplace of all creation. Their posture is simultaneously that of receiving the 'seed' of the male Sky and the 'birth-giving' posture as she causes all life to originate from her inexhaustible womb. The lotus for her head is the Earth-lotus (*bhu-padma*), as so characteristically symbolized in the Vedic and Puranic ontology (Agrawala, 1992 : 71).

10. Besides, some ritual vessels like a new type of bottle-necked jar (sprinkler) with additional perforation running through the neck upto the body (Fig. 12, Nos. 1-9) were obviously used for performing some rituals. Similar vessels occur at Kausambi and Sringaverapura in limited number. In addition the bottle-necked sprinkler commonly found in red polished ware at several sites in Gujarat (particularly Saurastra region) in a date range of 1st century BC—5th century AD was also found at the present site. As we have noted earlier (Singh, 1994 : 129), complete specimens of this type have been reported from Amreli, Yeleswaram, Kausambi and Kolhapur. Dhavalikar notes that imitation type of this vessel continued to occur till the 7th century AD as it is seen in sculptures and paintings. This vessel has also been depicted in the Ajanta paintings of Vakataka-Gupta date (5th century AD). It has been identified as *kundika*, a water vessel referred in the *Harsha-charita* of Banabhatta (Dhavalikar, 1998 : 140). It appears that Buddhist monks carried it as a water vessel and even Hieun Tsang in one picture is shown carrying it on his shoulder. The association of this vessel with Buddhism gets support from the fact that the Kausambi specimen comes from the Ghoshitarama monastery.

11. It needs to be emphasized that our three seasons' field investigation at Agiabir was only exploratory in nature. The main mound alone measures more than 2,5000 sq. m, of which less than 400 sq. m area could be investigated and the results amply testify to the potential of the site. We firmly believe that a horizontal excavation at Agiabir will provide a picture of stage-by-stage evolution of Indian culture in the Mid Ganga Valley.

Bibliography

Agarwal, D.P., 2000, *Ancient Metal Technology and Archaeology of South Asia*, New Delhi : Aryan Books International.

Agrawala, P.K., 1992, The Headless Nude Goddess and Her Identification, *Eastern Approaches: Essays on Asian Art & Archaeology* (ed.) T.S. Maxwell, New Delhi : Oxford University Press.

Banerjee, N.R., 1959, The Technique of Manufacture of Stone Beads in Ancient Ujjain, *Journal of the Asiatic Society* 1 (20): 179-198.

Basa, K.K. and S.S.M. Rahaman, 1998, Bronze Knobbed Bowls from Wari, Banglaesh: Implication for Trade, *Journal of Bengal Art* 3 : 291-98.

Chase, W.T., 1979, Solid Samples from Metallic Antiquities and their Examination, *Proceedings of Second ISCRP, Cultural Property and Analytical Chemistry* : 73-109.

Chaturvedi, S.N., 1985, Advances of Vindhyan Neolithic and Chalcolithic Culture to the Himalayan Terai, *Man & Environment* 9: 101-108.

Chakrabarti, D.K., 2001, *Archaeological Geography of the Ganga Plain*, New Delhi : Permanent Black.

Chattopadhyay, P.K., 1992, Archaeometallurgy in India : Studies on Technoculture in Early Copper and Iron Ages in Bihar and West Bengal, unpublished Ph.D. Thesis, Patna University.

Dhavalikar, M.K., 1998, *Historical Archaeology of India*, New Delhi : Books & Books.

Dhavalikar, M.K., H.D. Sankalia & Z.D. Desai, 1988, *Excavations at Inamgaon*, Vol. 2, Part II, Pune : Deccan College Postgraduate & Research Institute.

Francis, Peter, 1978-79, The Arecanut Bead: Is it a Bead?, *Puratattva* 10 : 95-99.

Gaur, R.C., 1983, *Excavations at Atranjikhera*, Delhi: Motilal Banarasidass.

Ghosh, A. (*Ed.*), 1989, *An Encyclopaedia of Indian Archaeology*, New Delhi: Munshiram Manoharlal Publisher Pvt. Ltd.

Gupta, H.P., 1976, Holocene Palynology from Meander Lake in the Ganga Valley, district Pratapgarh, UP, *The Palaeobotanist* 25 : 109-119.

IAR, *Indian Archaeology 1964-65 : A Review* : 42-43, New Delhi: Archaeological Survey of India.

Kenoyer, J.M., 1986, Indus Bead Industry : Contribution to Bead Technology, *Ornament* 10 (1) : 18-23.

Khadalavala, Karl, 1960, Brahmapuri : A Consideration of the Metal Objects Found in the Kunangar Hoard, *Lalit Kala* 7 : 27-95.

Kingery, W.D. and Pamela B. Vandiver, 1986, *Ceramic Masterpieces*, New York & London : 51-55.

Lal, B.B., 1993, *Excavations at Sringaverapura* 1977-86, New Delhi : Archaeological Survey of India,

Mackay, E.J.H., 1943, *Chanhudaro Excavations, 1935-36*, Boston : Boston Museum of Fine Arts.

Marshall, J., 1915, Excavations at Bhita, *Archaeological Survey of India : Annual Report, 1911-12* : 24-94.

——, 1951 (reprinted 1975), *Taxila*, 3 Vols., Delhi : Motilal Banarasidass.

Misra, B.B., 2000, Chalcolithic Culture of the Northern Vindhyas and Middle Ganga Valley, in *Peeping Through the Past : G.R. Sharma Memorial Volume* (eds.) S.C. Bhattacharya, V.D. Misra, J.N. Pandey and J.N. Pal (Allahabad), Department of Ancient History, Culture & Archeology, pp. 66-85.

Misra, V.D., 1988, Excavations at Damdama, Warikalan, Pratapgarh district, Uttar Pradesh, *Bulletin of Museum and Archaeology, U.P.*, pp. 41-42.

——, 1997a, The Mesolithic Cultures of the Vindhyas and the Ganga Valley with Special Reference to Environment and Archaeology, *Him-Kānti* (Prof. K.P. Nautiyal Felicitation Volume (eds.) B.M. Khanduri and Vinod Nautiyal, Delhi : Book India Publishing Co., pp. 41-42.

——, 1997b, *Some Aspects of Indian Archaeology*, Allahabad : Prabhat Prakashan.

——, 1999a, A Brief Note on Indian Stone Age Archaeology, *The Dawn of Indian Civilization (upto c. 600 BC)* (ed.) G.C. Pande, Vol. I, Part I, pp. 129-138.

——, 1999b, Agriculture, Domestication of Animals and Ceramic and Other Industries in Prehistoric India : Mesolithic and Neolithic, *The Dawn of Indian Civilization (upto c. 600 BC)* (ed.) G.C. Pande, Vol. I, Part I: 233-266.

Misra, V.D. and M.C. Gupta, 1995, Pre-NBPW Cultures in the Mid-Ganga Valley, *Prof. Agam Prasad Mathur Felicitation Volume*, Vol. III, Agra: Huzuri Bhavan, Peepal Mandi : 21-34.

Misra, V.D., B.B. Misra, J.N. Pandey and J.N. Pal, 1996, A Preliminary Report of Excavations at Jhusi, *Pragdhara* 6 : 63-66.

Misra, V.D., J.N. Pal and M.C. Gupta, 1999, Further Excavations at Jhusi, district Allahabad (Uttar Pradesh), *Pragdhara* 9 : 45-49.

——, 2000, Further Excavations at Jhusi (1998-99), district Allahabad (Uttar Pradesh), *Pragdhara* 10 : 23-30.

Misra, V.N., 2001, Prehistoric Human Colonization of India, *Journal of Biosciences 26* (4), Supplement : 491-531.

——, 2002, Keynote Address, *Mesolithic India* (eds.) V.D. Misra and J.N. Pal, Allahabad, University of Allahabad, 1-66.

Narain, A.K. and T.N. Roy, 1968, *The Excavations at Prahladpur*, Varanasi : Banaras Hindu University.

Narain, A.K. and P. Singh, 1977, *Excavations at Rajghat*, Part III, Varanasi : Banaras Hindu University.

Pal, J.N., 2002, The Mesolithic Phase in the Ganga Valley (ed.) K. Paddayya, *Recent Studies in Indian Archaeology*, ICHR Monograph Series No. 6, New Delhi, Munshiram Manoharlal Publisher Pvt. Ltd..

Pant, D.D. and Rekha Pant, 1980, Preliminary Observations of Pollen Flora of Chopani-Mando (Vindhyas) and Mahadaha (Ganga Valley), *Beginnings of Agriculture*, Allahabad : Avinash Prakashan.

Pathan, H., 1989, *Pratnatawick Nidarshan Wari Bateswar Narshingdi*, Granth Suhrid Prakashni (in Bangla).

Puri, K.N., 1998 (reprint), *Excavations at Rairh*, Jaipur : Publication Scheme.

Rajan, K. 1990, New Light on the Megalithic Culture of Kongu Region, Tamil Nadu, *Man & Environment* 15(1) : 93-102.

Rajpitak, W. and Neigel J. Seeley, 1979, The Bronze Bowls from Ban Don Ta Phet, Thailand : An Enigma of Prehistoric Metallurgy, *World Archaeology* 11 (1) : 26-31.

Rao, S.R., 1973, *Lothal and the Indus Civilization*, Bombay : Asia Publishing House.

Roy, T.N., 1983, *The Ganges Civilization*, New Delhi : Ramanand Vidya Bhawan.

Saraswat, K.S., N.K. Sharma and D.C. Saini, 1994, Plant Economy at Ancient Narhan, in P. Singh, *Excavations at Narhan (1984-89)*, Varanasi & New Delhi : Banaras Hindu University and B.R. Publishing Corporation.

Sharma, G.R., 1969, *Excavations at Kausambi 1949-50*, Memoirs of the Archaeological Survey of India, No. 74.

Sharma, G.R., V.D. Misra, D. Mandal and J.N. Pal, 1980, *Beginnings of Agriculture*, Allahabad : Avinash Prakashan,

Sharma, G.R., V.D. Misra, D. Mandal, B.B. Misra and J.N. Pal, 1980, From Hunting and Food-Gathering to Domestication of Plants and Animals-Epi-Palaeolithiic to Neolithic-Excavation at Chopani Mando, Mahadaha and Mahagara, *History and Archaeology*, I, Allahabad University.

Sharma, S., M. Joachimski, M. Sharma, H.J. Tobschall, I.B. Singh, C. Sharma, M.S. Chauhan and G. Morgenroth, 2000, Holocene Palaeoclimate Reconstruction Using Multiproxy Data from Sanai Lake, Central Ganga Plain, India, *Quaternary Science Review* (in press)

——, 2003, Monsoon Variability, Vegetation Change and Human Inhabitation Over 15,000 Years from Multi Proxy Record of a Lake Deposit in Ganga Plain, India, Terra Nova (in press).

Singh, A.K., 1999, Explorations at Agiabir, district-Mirzapur (U.P.), *Pragdhara* 9 : 51-56.

——, 2001, Agiabir ke Vastu Avashesh, *Pragdhara*, 11 : 201-205.

Singh, A.K. and P.K. Chattopadhyay, 2002, In Search of High Tin Bronze, *Puratattva* 32 : 101-106.

Singh, A.K. and S.K. Singh, 2000, Importance of Bead Manufacturing Workshop at Agiabir, Distt. Mirzapur, Uttar Pradesh, *Bharati* 24, (Pts. I & II) : 141-149.

Singh, B.P., 1989, Khairadih : A Chalcolithic Settlement, *Puratattva* 18 : 28-34.

——, 1990, Early Farming Communities of Kaimur Foot Hills, *Puratattva* 19 : 6-18.

Singh, Indra Bir, 1996, Geological Evolution of Ganga Plain—An Overview, *Journal of Palaeontological Society of India*, 41, 99-137.

Singh, P., 1994, *Excavations at Narhan (1984-89),*), Varanasi and New Delhi : Banaras Hindu University and B.R. Publishing Corporation.

——, 1993, Archaeological Excavations at Imlidih Khurd"1992, *Pragdhara* 3 : 21-36.

——, 1994, Further Excavations at Imlidih Khurd, *Pragdhara* 4 : 41-48.

——, 1996, Prelude to Urbanization in the Sarayupar Plain, *Presidential Address to the Indian History Congress*, 57 Session, Chennai.

Singh, P. and A.K. Singh, 1995, Protohistoric Investigations in Ballia district, *Pragdhara* 5 : 21-36.

Singh, P. and A.K. Singh, 1998, Excavations at Bhunadih, district-Ballia (UP), *Pragdhara* 8 : 12-29.

——, 1999, Agiabir—1999 : A Preliminary Report, *Puratattva* 29 : 117-119.

——, 2000, Excavations at Agiabir, district Mirzapur (UP), *Pragdhara* 10 : 31-55.

——, 2001, Second Season at Agiabir : A Note, *Puravritta*, 1 : 157-159.

——, 2001, A Rare Discovery of Metal Objects from Agiabir, district-Mirzapur, Uttar Pradesh, *Man & Environment*, 26 (2) : 109-115.

Singh, P., A.K. Singh and B. Singh, 1996, Excavations at Waina, district-Ballia, *Pragdhara* 6 : 41-61.

Singh, R.L., 1971, *India : A Regional Geography*, Varanasi, Banaras Hindu University; National Geographical Society of India

Singh, R.N. and S. Singh, 2000, Characterization of Faience Beads from Agiabir, *Pragdhara*, 10 : 65-68.

Singh, S.C., 1965, Delimination of the Middle Ganga Plain, *The National Geographical Journal of India*, Varanasi : Banaras Hindu University : 74-83.

Singh, S.K., 2000, Lithic Industry of Agiabir, district Mirzapur (UP), *Pragdhara*, 10 : 57-63.

Spate, O.H.K., 1954, *India and Pakistan : A Regional Geography*, London.

Stamp, Sir Dudley, 1967, *Asia : A Regional and Economic Geography*, London, Methuen & Co. Twelfth Edition.

Tewari, R., 1997, Excavations at Raja-Nala-Ka-Tila (1995-96), district Sonbhadra (UP) : Preliminary Observations, *Pragdhara* 7 : 77-95.

——, 1998, Excavations at Raja-Nala-Ka-Tila (1996-97), district Sonbhadra (UP) : Preliminary Observations, *Pragdhara* 8 : 99-105.

——, 1998, In Quest of Early Iron Age Sites in Karmanasa Valley, *Pragdhara* 8: 57-67.

——, 2001, Antiquity of Iron in South-Eastern Uttar Pradesh, *Bharati*, 25 : 124-137.

Tewari R., R.K. Srivastava, K.K. Singh, 2002, Excavation at Lahuradewa, district Sant Kabir Nagar, U.P., *Puratattva*, 32 : 54-62.

Tewari, R., R.K. Srivastava, K.S. Saraswat and K.K. Singh, 2000, Excavations at Malhar, District Chandauli (UP) 1999 : A Preliminary Report, *Pragdhara* 10 : 69-98.

Tewari, R., P.C. Pant, I.B. Singh, S. Sharma, M. Sharma, P. Srivastava, A.K. Singhvi, P.K. Mira and H.J. Tobschall, 2002, Middle Palaeolithic Human Activity and Palaeoclimate at Kalpi in Yamuna Valley, Ganga Plain, *Man & Environment* 27, No. 2 : 1-13.

Tewari Rakesh, R.K. Srivastava, K.K. Singh, K.S. Saraswat, I.B. Singh, 2003, 'Preliminary Report of the Excavation at Lahuradewa, District Sant Kabir Nagar, UP, 2001-2002: Wider Archaeological Implications', *Pragdhara* 13 (in press).

Thaplyal, K.K., 1972, *Studies in Ancient Indian Seals*, Lucknow : Akhil Bharatiya Sanskrit Parishad.

Thomas, P.K., 1979, Role of Animals in the Food Economy of the Mesolithic Cultures of the Western and Central India, *A Source Book of Indian Archaeology*, (eds.) F.R. Allchin and D.K. Chakrabarti, Delhi.

Thomas, P.K., P.P. Joglekar, V.D. Misra, J.N. Pandey and J.N. Pal, 1995, Faunal Evidence for the Mesolithic Food Economy of the Gangetic Plain with Special Reference to Damdama, *Bio-Archaeology of Mesolithic India : An Integrated Approach*: 322-28.

——, 1996, Faunal Evidence for the Mesolithic Food Economy of the Gangetic Plain with Special Reference to Damdama, in *Bio-Archaeology of Mesolithic India : An Integrated Approach*, Colloquium XXXIII of the International Union of Prehistoric and Protohistoric Sciences (G.D. Afanas'ev, S. Cleuziou, J.R. Lukacs and M. Tosi, eds.), 255-66. Forli : ABACO Edizioni.

Tite, M.S., I.C. Freestone and M, Bimson, 1983, Egyptian Faience : An Investigation of the Methods of Production, *Archaeometry*, 25 (1) : 17-27.

Tosi, M.L. Bondioli and M. Vidale, 1984, Craft Activity Areas and Survey at Mohenjodaro, *Interim Report* 1: 9-37. Aschen, RWTH ISMEO.

Varma, R.K., 1999, The Emergence of Culture in the Vindhya-Ganga Region with Special Reference to Old Stone Age, *The Dawn of Indian Civilization (upto c. 600 BC)* (ed.) G.C. Pande, Vol. I, Part I: 175-204.

Varma, R.K., V.D. Misra, J.N. Pandey and J.N. Pal, 1985, Preliminary Report on the Excavation at Damdama (1982-84), *Man & Environment*, 11.

Vats, M.S., 1940, (reprint 1997), *Excavation at Harappa*, Vols. I & II. New Delhi: Munshiram Manoharlal Publishers Pvt. Ltd.

Wheeler, R.E.M., 1946, Archaeological Fieldwork in India : Planning Ahead, *Ancient India* 5 : 4-11.

Wheeler, R.E.M., A. Ghosh and Krishna Deva, 1946, Arikamedu : An Indo-Roman Trading Station on the East Coast of India, *Ancient India* 2 : 17-124.

Wulff, H.E., H.S. Wulff and L. Koch, 1968, Egyptian Faience : A Possible Survival in Iran, *Archaeology* 21 : 98-107.

Yasuda, Yoshinori (ed.), 2002, *The Origins of Pottery and Agriculture*, New Delhi : Roli Books.

Index

Akahua 12
Allahabad 4, 6, 7, 12, 23, 67, 89
Arikamedu 72
Arun Kosi 4
Atranjikhera 34, 77

Babul 5
Baghor II 7
Balan 4
Banabhatta 83
Banaras 6, 7, 23
Banerjee, N.R. 72
Banki 7
Banwarighat 12
Banyan 5
Baragaon 12
Barhandi 4
Baruna 4
Basa, K.K. 62
Bataubir 5
Belan 5, 6
Belrahi 5
Besu 4
Bhelwani 12
Bhotia Kosi 4
Bon Don Ta Phet 62
Brahmapuri 60

Chadraketugarh 62
Chandatari 5
Chandauli 6, 19
Chandraketugarh 60
Chanhu-Daro 72
Chase, W.T. 62
Chattopadhyay, P.K. 62
Chechar-Kutubpur 10, 12
Chhoti Saryu 4
Chilbil 5
Chopani Mando 7, 8

Damdama 7, 8, 9
Dhak 5
Dhaṅuhi 7
Dhavalikar, M.K. 33, 83
Dhuriapar 12, 19, 81
Dhusan 4
Dudh Kosi 4
Dudley Stamp 1

Francis, Peter 74

Gandak 3, 4
Gandak System 3, 4
Gandak-Kosi 2
Gangi 4
Gaur, R.C. 77
Ghaghara 2, 3, 4, 19
Ghagharia 7
Gharwa 6
Ghosh, A. 58, 60
Gomati 2, 4
Gularihwaghat 12

Hajipur 4
Hāndā 50, 52
Hāndī 41, 50, 51, 56, 58, 63
Harappa 60, 75
Hippo 5

Imlidih Khurd 10, 12, 13, 19, 34, 81

Jaunpur 7, 12
Jhusi 12, 15, 17, 40, 52, 67, 82, 83

Kaitha 5
Kalpi 6
Kamauli 12
Kamla 4
Karagola 4
Karmnasa 2, 5
Kausambi 19, 40, 67, 82, 83
Kenoyer, J.M. 72
Khairadih 12, 14, 19, 34
Khandalavala 60
Khutabir 5
Kingery, W.D. 74
Kodumanal 72
Kosi System 3, 4
Kosi-Mahananda 2
Kundangar 60
Kurha 6

Lahariadih 7
Lahuradeva 10, 11, 12, 13, 15
Lal, B.B. 40
Likhu Kosi 4
Lisora 5
Lota 13, 28, 33, 50, 51, 56, 81
Lothal 72
Lukacs, J.R. 9

Mackay, E.J.H. 72
Madhauli 7
Mahadaha 7, 8, 9
Mahagara 6
Mahasthangarh 60, 62
Mahi 5
Mahua 5
Malhar 12, 15, 16, 19, 81
Mandah 6
Mangai 4
Marshall, J. 40, 60, 62, 83
Marwa 5
Mason Dih 12, 58, 60
Mirzapur 6, 23
Mohenjo-daro 72
Mortimer, Sir Wheeler 1
Murli Mahugarh 5

Nahusa Raja Ka Tila 12
Narain, A.K. 38, 51, 58, 68
Narhan 12, 13, 14, 19, 23, 28, 30, 34, 52, 58, 60, 62, 63, 77, 81
Narshingdi 62
Naunkalan 5
Neem 5

Paisara 9
Pakar 5
Pal, J.N. 5
Pant, D.D. 5
Pathan, H. 62
Pelkhawar 12
Perkin Elmer 62
Pipal 5
Prahladpur 12, 13, 38, 78
Pratapgarh 7, 12
Pure Deojani 12
Puri, K.N. 62

Raja-Nala-Ka-Tila 12, 15, 19, 81
Rajan, K. 72
Rajghat 12
Rajpitak, W 62
Ramgarh 5
Ramnagarghat 12
Rao, S.R. 72
Rhino 5
Roy, T.N. 38, 51, 58, 68

Salhipur 6
Sant Kabir Nagar 10, 12
Saptgandaki 4

Sarai Nahar Rai 7, 8, 9
Sarai-Mohana 12
Saraswat, K.S. 14
Saura 4
Senuwar 10, 11, 12, 13, 14
Sharma, N.K. 40, 72
Sheesham 5
Siras 5
Sirkap 60
Sohgaura 10, 12, 14
Son valley 2, 5, 6
Sonbhadra 6, 7, 12, 19
Sravasti 19
Sringaverapura 13, 40, 67, 83
Sugarus 4
Suleman Parvatpur 6
Sultanpur 7
Sun Kosi 4
Susipar 12

Tamarind 5
Tamba Kosi 4
Tamber Kosi 4
Taradih 10, 12, 13
Taxila 60, 62, 82
Tewari, R. 3, 6, 11, 19
Thali 81
Thaplyal, K.K. 68
Thomas, P.K. 7
Tilaleh 4
Tite, M.S. 76
Tons 4, 5
Tosi, M.L. Bondioli 72

Ujjain 72

Vandiver, P.B. 74
Varma, R.K. 5, 7, 8, 9
Vats, M.S. 60

Waina 12, 13, 19, 81
Wari-Bateswar 62
Wheeler, R.E.M. 1, 72

Yangtze valley 10
Yasuda, Yoshinori 10